Check and test

Maths

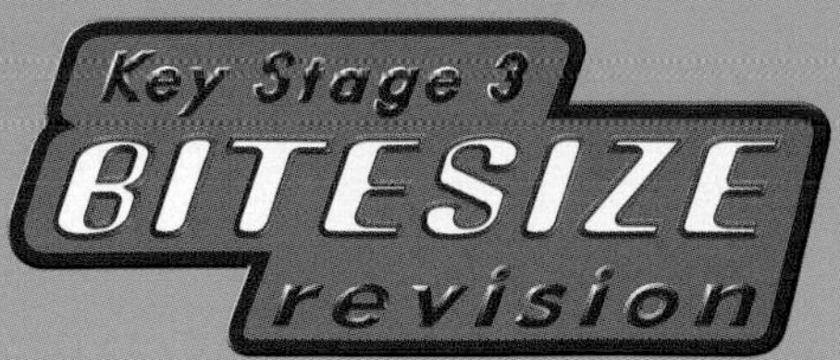

Check and test

Maths

Dr Naomi Norman

Published by BBC Educational Publishing,
BBC White City, 201 Wood Lane, London W12 7TS

First published 2001

ISBN 0563 54355 3

Illustrations by Hardlines Ltd
Colour reproduction by Spectrum Colour, England
Printed and bound by Poligrafico Dehoniano, Italy

Contents

Shape and space

Angles and lines

2-D shapes and 3-D solids

Symmetry, congruence and translation

Enlargement

Measure

Units of measure

Perimeter, area and volume

Loci

Handling data

Representing and interpreting data

Comparing distributions

Probability

Mental maths

About KS3 Bitesize

KS3 Bitesize is a revision service designed to help you achieve success in the National Tests. There are books, television programmes and a website at **www.bbc.co.uk/education/revision**. The service is called *Bitesize* because it breaks revision into bite-sized chunks, making it easier for you to learn. *Check and Test* is the latest addition to the *Bitesize* revision service.

How to use this book

This book is divided into the 100 essential things you need to know, so your revision is quick and simple. It provides a quick test for each bite-sized chunk so you can check that you know it!

Use this book to check your understanding of KS3 Maths. If you can prove to yourself that you're confident with these key ideas, you'll know that you're on track with your learning.

You can use this book to test yourself:

- during your KS3 course
- at the end of the course during revision.

As you revise, you can use *Check and Test* in several ways:

- as a summary of the essential information on each of the 100 topics to help you revise those areas
- to check your revision progress: test yourself to see how confident you are with each topic
- to keep track and plan your time: you can aim to check and test a set number of topics each time you revise, knowing how many you need to cover in total and how much time you've got.

Other Bitesize resources

Key Stage 3 Bitesize Revision: Maths is a book that contains the key information and skills you need to revise, plus lots of tips and practice questions to help you improve your results. ISBN: 0 563 47431 9

The KS3 Bitesize Revision: Maths website provides even more practice and explanation to help you revise. It can be found at **www.bbc.co.uk/education/revision**

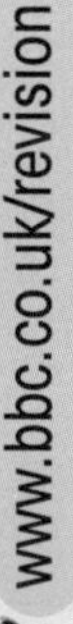

Topic checker

Use the topic checkers on this page to keep track of the topics you've covered as you work through them. They're also useful to double-check that you've covered each area.

- Once you're confident with a topic and can answer the questions, you can cross the topic number off the first grid. As you check the topic for a second or third time, you can cross it off each grid.
- You'll be able to see which topics you've covered most thoroughly and those which you haven't done as much work on. Is this because you're confident that you know these topics or are you putting off looking at them?
- Any problem topics should sink in by your third check.
- Don't worry if you don't have time to go over each topic three times. Every time you look at a topic, you'll be able to remember a little bit more.

First time

1	2	3	4	5	6	7	8	9	10
11	12	13	14	15	16	17	18	19	20
21	22	23	24	25	26	27	28	29	30
31	32	33	34	35	36	37	38	39	40
41	42	43	44	45	46	47	48	49	50
51	52	53	54	55	56	57	58	59	60
61	62	63	64	65	66	67	68	69	70
71	72	73	74	75	76	77	78	79	80
81	82	83	84	85	86	87	88	89	90
91	92	93	94	95	96	97	98	99	100

Second time

1	2	3	4	5	6	7	8	9	10
11	12	13	14	15	16	17	18	19	20
21	22	23	24	25	26	27	28	29	30
31	32	33	34	35	36	37	38	39	40
41	42	43	44	45	46	47	48	49	50
51	52	53	54	55	56	57	58	59	60
61	62	63	64	65	66	67	68	69	70
71	72	73	74	75	76	77	78	79	80
81	82	83	84	85	86	87	88	89	90
91	92	93	94	95	96	97	98	99	100

Third time

1	2	3	4	5	6	7	8	9	10
11	12	13	14	15	16	17	18	19	20
21	22	23	24	25	26	27	28	29	30
31	32	33	34	35	36	37	38	39	40
41	42	43	44	45	46	47	48	49	50
51	52	53	54	55	56	57	58	59	60
61	62	63	64	65	66	67	68	69	70
71	72	73	74	75	76	77	78	79	80
81	82	83	84	85	86	87	88	89	90
91	92	93	94	95	96	97	98	99	100

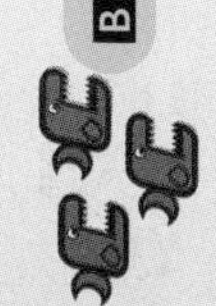

Place value

Check the facts

0, 1, 2, 3, 4, 5, 6, 7, 8, 9 are all digits.

The place of each digit in a number tells you its value.

The place of the right-hand digit tells you how many **units** there are.

The place of the next digit to the left tells you how many **tens.**

The place of the next digit to the left tells you how many **hundreds.**

And so on . . . **thousands**

. . . tens of thousands.

Example: 7206

(Seven thousand two hundred and fifty-six has **four digits.**)

The place of the 6 tells you there are six **units.**
The place of the 0 tells you there are no **tens.**
The place of the 2 tells you there are two **hundreds.**
The place of the 7 tells you there are seven **thousands.**

You can write this number in columns or as a sum:

thousands	hundreds	tens	units		
7	2	0	6	=	7000 + 200 + 0 + 6

Test yourself

1 a) How many tens in the number 676?
b) How many hundreds in the number 3143?
c) How many hundreds in the number 8056?

2 a) Write this number in digits: four thousand six hundred and one.
b) Write this number in digits: twelve thousand and fifty-seven.

3 Look at these six digits: 5 7 1 8 6 0
a) Use the digits to make a four-digit number smaller than one thousand five hundred and eight. (You can only use each digit once.)
b) Use the digits to make the biggest four-digit number possible. (Again, you can only use each digit once.)

Check the facts

Some addition and subtraction calculations can be done in your head.

Example: Adding pairs of numbers that total 100:

$28 + 72 = 100$ $54 + 46 = 100$

More difficult addition and subtraction calculations can be done using pen and paper.

Examples:

Calculate: 3617 + 921

```
   3617
+   921
   ----
   4538
   1
```

Calculate: 2075 − 83

```
  ¹2̸ ⁹0̸ ¹7 5
−         8 3
  -----------
   1  9  9 2
```

Remember: for addition and subtraction calculations, line up digits so that units, tens, hundreds . . . each have their own column.

Begin by adding or subtracting the units column.

Know how to carry digits. You will need to carry:

- when **adding**, if the digits in a column add up to more than 9
- when **subtracting**, if you have to subtract a bigger digit from a smaller digit in a column.

Don't forget to show all your working!

Test yourself

1 Calculate in your head:

a) 7 + 13 b) 16 − 9 c) 34 − 5

d) 35 + 52 e) 77 + 14 f) 100 − 62

2 Calculate using pen and paper, showing all your working:

a) 134 + 5615 b) 4160 − 328 c) 2066 − 79

Did you get any answers wrong? To get more practice, make up calculations of your own and check the answers on a calculator.

3 Coral and her brother stand on a set of bathroom scales. Together they weigh 100 kg. Coral weighs 43 kg. What does her brother weigh?

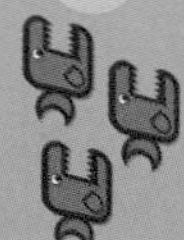

Check the facts

Know all your times tables up to 10 x 10.

- To work out more difficult multiplication calculations, use a pen and paper and work in columns:

```
  3 7 4
×     8
-------
2 9 9 2
  5 3
```

Look! $4 \times 8 = 32$
So, 3 has to be carried into the next column.
$7 \times 8 = 56$, add the 3 makes 59.
So, 5 has to be carried into the next column.
$3 \times 8 = 24$, add the 5 makes 29.
So the answer is **2992**.

- To work out even more difficult multiplication calculations you can use the method called **long multiplication**:

```
    6 1 9
  ×   5 3
---------
  1 8 5 7
      2
3 0 9 5 0
    4
---------
3 2 8 0 7
```

$619 \times 3 = 1857$

$619 \times 50 = 30\,950$
(write the 0, then work out $619 \times 5 = 3095$)
Now add: $619 \times 3 = 1857$
$+\ 619 \times 50 = 30\,950$
$619 \times 53 = 32\,807$

You may know another method of multiplication. If so, work out **374 × 8** and **619 × 53**. Do you get the answers **2992** and **32 807**?

Test yourself

1 Calculate in your head:

a) 4×6 c) 9×7 e) 4×8
b) 8×5 d) 6×7 f) 7×8

If you were unsure of any of the answers, learn your times tables and ask somebody to test you on your way to school.

2 Calculate, showing all your working:

a) 841×6 c) 277×83 e) 149×31
b) 569×2 d) 785×56 f) 328×429

Did you get any answers wrong? To get more practice, make up calculations of your own and check the answers on a calculator.

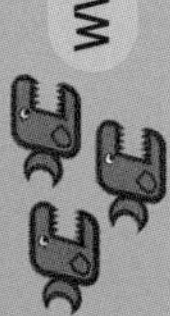

Check the facts

If you know your times tables up to 10 x 10, you will be able to do the following division calculations in your head:

$35 \div 5$ $48 \div 8$ $72 \div 9$

Were your answers: $35 \div 5 = 7$, $48 \div 8 = 6$, $72 \div 9 = 8$?
If not, then you need to practise your times tables!

To work out more difficult division calculations, use a pen and paper and show your working like this:

$$\begin{array}{r} 1\ 5\ 9 \\ 4\ \overline{)\,6\ {}^{2}3\ {}^{3}6} \end{array}$$

Look! 4 into 6 goes 1, remainder 2.
So the remainder 2 has to be carried.
4 into 23 goes 5, remainder 3.
So the remainder 3 has to be carried.
4 into 36 goes 9. **Answer:** 159

To work out even more difficult division calculations, you can use the method called **long division**:

$$\begin{array}{r} 27 \\ 15\ \overline{)\,405} \\ \underline{30} \\ 105 \\ \underline{105} \\ 0 \end{array}$$

15 does not go into 4, so look at 40.
Consider the 15 times table and find the biggest number that is less than 40.
That is $15 \times 2 = 30$. So, 15 into 40 goes 2.
Find the remainder by working out $40 - 30$.
Bring down the 5.
Consider the 15 times table and find the biggest number that is less than 105.
$15 \times 7 = 105$. So, 15 into 105 goes 7.
There is no remainder. **Answer:** 27

Test yourself

1 Calculate in your head:

a) $36 \div 6$ c) $32 \div 4$ e) $42 \div 7$
b) $54 \div 9$ d) $40 \div 8$ f) $56 \div 8$

If you were unsure of any of the answers, learn your times tables and then ask somebody to test you on your way to school.

2 Calculate, showing all your working:

a) $702 \div 9$ c) $4865 \div 5$ e) $726 \div 22$
b) $2304 \div 6$ d) $525 \div 25$ f) $2211 \div 33$

Did you get any answers wrong? To get more practice, make up calculations of your own and check the answers on a calculator.

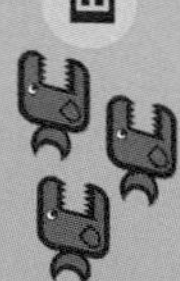

Word problems

Check the facts

Word problems do not tell you what maths operation to use. You have to read the problem and decide whether to add, subtract, divide or multiply.

Remember: the information in a word problem is given for a reason, so don't ignore it. Read it twice.

Example:

Judy, Jack and Jill are counting traffic passing their school. Judy counts 8 lorries. Jack counts half as many bicycles as lorries. Jill counts three times as many cars as lorries. How many lorries, bicycles and cars pass by?

Judy counted 8 lorries.
Jack counted half as many bicycles, that's $\frac{1}{2}$ of $8 = 4$.
Jill counted three times as many cars, that's $3 \times 8 = 24$.
So, lorries, bicycles and cars = $\mathbf{8 + 4 + 24 = 36}$.

Sometimes words in a problem may give clues:

- 'three **times** as many cars' suggests **multiply**
- 'lorries, bicycles **and** cars' suggests add.

Always check your answer to make sure it makes sense!

Test yourself

1 Jill and her mum share the same birthday. They were both born on 29 January.

a) Jill was 10 years old on 29 January 1999. How old will she be on 29 January 2010?

b) Jill's mum was four times Jill's age on 29 January 1999. What year was Jill's mum born?

c) How old will Jill's mum be on 29 January 2015?

2 A group of 23 tourists want to travel by taxi from Heathrow Airport to their hotel in Central London. Each taxi can carry four people.

a) How many taxis do the tourists need?

b) Each taxi costs £25.30. What is the total cost of the taxi rides?

c) The tourists want to share the cost of the taxis equally. How much must each tourist pay?

Check the facts

Factors

A factor of a whole number is any whole number that divides exactly into it (with no remainder).

Example: Factors of 12 are **1**, **2**, **3**, 4, **6**, 12.
Factors of 30 are **1**, **2**, **3**, 5, **6**, 10, 15, 30.

The **highest common factor** (hcf) is the largest number that divides exactly into two or more numbers.

The factors that are highlighted are the **common factors** of 12 and 30 (they are the factors that appear in both lists). The highest common factor is 6.

Multiples

When a whole number is multiplied by another whole number, the answer is a multiple of both numbers.

Example: Multiples of 4 are 4, 8, **12**, 16, 20, **24**, 28 . . .
Multiples of 6 are 6, **12**, 18, **24**, 30, 36, 42 . . .

The **lowest common multiple** (lcm) is the smallest number that two or more numbers will divide into.

The **common multiples** of 4 and 6 are highlighted (they are the multiples that appear in both lists). The lowest common multiple is 12.

Test yourself

1 List the factors of these numbers:

a) 15 b) 28 c) 24 d) 35

What is the highest common factor of:

e) 15 and 35? f) 24 and 28?

2 Look at these six numbers:

36	27	30	72	60	18

Which numbers are multiples of:

a) 2? b) 6? c) 9? d) 10?

Which number is the lowest common multiple of:

e) 6 and 9? f) 6 and 10?

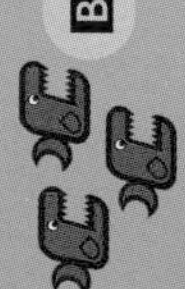

Prime, square and cube numbers

Check the facts

Prime numbers

A **prime number** is a whole number that has only two factors: 1 and itself.

Example: 2, 3, 5, 7, 11, 13, 17, 19

1 is not a prime number, as it has only one factor: 1

Square numbers

When a number is multiplied by itself, the answer is a **square number**.

Example: $1 \times 1 = 1$ $2 \times 2 = 4$ $3 \times 3 = 9$
$4 \times 4 = 16$ $5 \times 5 = 25$

So, 1, 4, 9, 16, 25 are all **square numbers**.

Square numbers make squares: 1 4 9

Cube numbers

When a number is multiplied by itself three times, the answer is a **cube number**.

Example: $1 \times 1 \times 1 = 1$ $2 \times 2 \times 2 = 8$ $3 \times 3 \times 3 = 27$
$4 \times 4 \times 4 = 64$ $5 \times 5 \times 5 = 125$

So, 1, 8, 27, 64, 125 are all **cube numbers**.

Cube numbers make cubes:

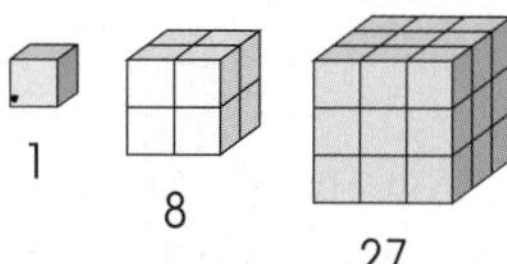

Test yourself

1 a) What is the next prime number after 19?
b) What is the smallest prime number?
c) What is the next square number after 25?
d) What is the next cube number after 27?
e) What is the highest square number less than 99?

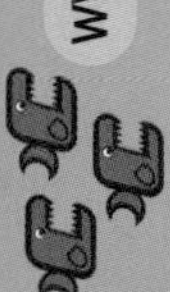

Check the facts

Powers

$3 \times 3 = 9$ may be written as $\mathbf{3^2}$. This is **3 squared**.

3^2 may be read as **3 to the power of 2** or **3 to the order 2**.

All numbers to the power or order of 2 are squared numbers.

$4 \times 4 \times 4 = 64$ may be written as $\mathbf{4^3}$. This is **4 cubed**.

4^3 may be read as **4 to the power of 3** or **4 to the order 3**.

All numbers to the power or order of 3 are cubed numbers.

$6 \times 6 \times 6 \times 6 \times 6 = 7776$ may be written as $\mathbf{6^5}$.

6^5 may be read as **6 to the power of 5** or **6 to the order 5**.

The big number that comes first is called the **base**.
The small number is the power, order or **index number**.
Numbers written like this are in **index form**.

The power, order or index number tells you how many times to multiply the base.

Use carefully!	4^2 is $4 \times 4 = 16$ ✔	4^2 is *not* $4 \times 2 = 8$ ✘

Square roots

A **square root** is the opposite of squared.

The square root of **9** is 3, as $3 \times 3 = 3^2 = 9$.

The square root of **25** is 5, as $5 \times 5 = 5^2 = 25$.

Square roots are written √, so $\sqrt{9} = 3$ and $\sqrt{25} = 5$.

Use carefully!	$\sqrt{4}$ is $\sqrt{4} = 2$ ✔	$\sqrt{4}$ is *not* $\sqrt{4} = 16$ ✘

Test yourself

1 Calculate:
a) 4^2 b) 3^3 c) 9^2

2 Write in index form:
a) $5 \times 5 \times 5 \times 5 \times 5$
b) $7 \times 7 \times 7 \times 7 \times 7$
c) $10 \times 10 \times 10 \times 10$
d) $3 \times 3 \times 3 \times 3 \times 3 \times 3 \times 3$

3 Find the roots of:
a) $\sqrt{100}$ b) $\sqrt{49}$ c) $\sqrt{36}$ d) $\sqrt{16}$ e) $\sqrt{4}$ f) $\sqrt{81}$ g) $\sqrt{64}$ h) $\sqrt{25}$

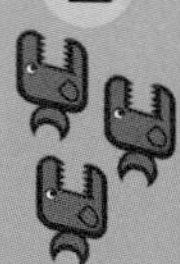

Multiplying by 10, 100 and 1000

Check the facts

Multiply by 10 by moving each digit one place to the left and putting one zero (0) on the end:

	thousands	hundreds	tens	units
			1	2
12 × 10 = 120		1	2	0

Multiply by 100 by moving each digit two places to the left and putting two zeros (0) on the end:

	thousands	hundreds	tens	units
			2	5
25 × 100 = 2500	2	5	0	0

Multiply by 1000 by moving each digit three places to the left and putting three zeros (0) on the end:

	thousands	hundreds	tens	units
				3
3 × 1000 = 3000	3	0	0	0

Examples:

16 × 10 = 160
16 × 100 = 1600
16 × 1000 = 16 000

52 × 10 = 520
52 × 100 = 5200
52 × 1000 = 52 000

Remember: multiply two numbers bigger than 1 and your answer will be bigger than the numbers with which you started.

Test yourself

1 Calculate:

a) 24 × 10
b) 7 × 100
c) 9 × 1000
d) 35 × 100
e) 82 × 10
f) 40 × 100

2 Fill in the gaps with the correct number: 10, 100 or 1000.

a) 4 × _____ = 400
b) 17 × _____ = 1700
c) 32 × _____ = 320
d) 5 × _____ = 5000
e) 43 × _____ = 4300
f) 1 × _____ = 1000

Did you get any answers wrong? To get more practice, make up calculations of your own and check the answers on a calculator.

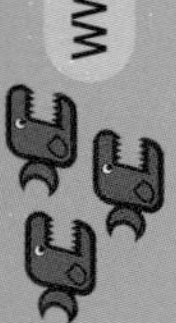

Dividing by 10, 100 and 1000

Check the facts

Divide by 10 by moving each digit one place to the right and cross one zero (0) off the end:

	thousands	hundreds	tens	units
		6	1	0
610 ÷ 10 = 61			6	1

Divide by 100 by moving each digit two places to the right and crossing two zeros (0) off the end:

	thousands	hundreds	tens	units
	5	4	0	0
5400 ÷ 100 = 54			5	4

Divide by 1000 by moving each digit three places to the right and crossing three zeros (0) off the end:

	thousands	hundreds	tens	units
	8	0	0	0
8000 ÷ 1000 = 8				8

Examples:

5000 ÷ 10 = 500
5000 ÷ 100 = 50
5000 ÷ 1000 = 5

12 000 ÷ 10 = 1200
12 000 ÷ 100 = 120
12 000 ÷ 1000 = 12

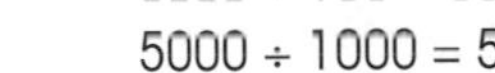

Test yourself

1 Calculate:

a) 360 ÷ 10
b) 33 000 ÷ 100
c) 9000 ÷ 1000
d) 5050 ÷ 10
e) 2000 ÷ 100
f) 3300 ÷ 10

2 Fill in the gaps with the correct number: 10, 100 or 1000.

a) 830 ÷ _____ = 83
b) 2900 ÷ _____ = 290
c) 1000 ÷ _____ = 10
d) 4000 ÷ _____ = 4
e) 100 ÷ _____ = 1
f) 7000 ÷ _____ = 70

Did you get any answers wrong? To get more practice, make up calculations of your own and check the answers on a calculator.

3 There are Grandma, Grandad, Mum, Dad and six children in the Polaz family. The Polaz family win £4500 in a competition and divide the money equally. How much do they each receive?

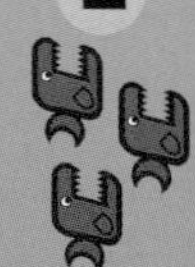

11 Multiplying and dividing by multiples of 10, 100 and 1000

Check the facts

Remember: when a whole number is multiplied by another whole number, the answer is a multiple of both numbers.

Multiples of 10 are 10, 20, 30, 40, 50 . . .
Multiples of 100 are 100, 200, 300, 400, 500 . . .
Multiples of 1000 are 1000, 2000, 3000, 4000, 5000 . . .

Multiply by multiples of 10, 100 and 1000 like this:
$20 \times 400 = (2 \times 10) \times (4 \times 100) = 2 \times 4 \times 10 \times 100$

Multiply the 2 by the 4:	$2 \times 4 = 8$
Multiply the 10 by the 100:	$10 \times 100 = 1000$
Now multiply the 8 by the 1000:	$8 \times 1000 = 8000$
So, the answer is $20 \times 400 = 8000$	

Divide by multiples of 10, 100 and 1000 like this:
$12\,000 \div 30 = (12 \times 1000) \div (3 \times 10) = 12 \div 3 \times 1000 \div 10$

Divide the 12 by the 3:	$12 \div 3 = 4$
Divide the 1000 by the 10:	$1000 \div 10 = 100$
Now multiply the 4 by the 100:	$4 \times 100 = 400$
So, the answer is $12\,000 \div 30 = 400$	

Test yourself

1 Calculate:

a) 200×30
b) 50×500
c) 600×40
d) 600×20
e) $15\,000 \div 500$
f) $9000 \div 30$
g) 900×50
h) $32\,000 \div 80$
i) 20×90

2 Fill in the gaps:

a) $400 \times$ _____ $= 16\,000$
b) _____ $\times 70 = 1400$
c) $24\,000 \div$ _____ $= 40$
d) _____ $\div 50 = 30$
e) $3000 \div$ _____ $= 60$
f) _____ $\times 50 = 1000$

3 Toby completes a 60-mile cycle ride for charity. Tina sponsored him 30p per mile. How much money (in pounds) must Toby collect from Tina?

What is a negative number?

Check the facts

Numbers above zero (0) are positive numbers.

Positive numbers are written with no sign or a **positive sign** (+) in front of them, like this:

56, +4, +610, 23, 102

Numbers below zero (0) are negative numbers.

Negative numbers are always written with a **negative sign** (–) in front of them, like this:

–6, –73, –2, –1671, –718

It is sometimes useful to think of numbers on a line:

–7 –6 –5 –4 –3 –2 –1 0 1 2 3 4 5 6 7

Positive numbers get bigger the further you move to the right of zero:

–5 –4 –3 –2 –1 0 1 2 3 4 5

numbers get bigger →

So, 2 is smaller than 5 and +4 is bigger than +3.

Negative numbers get smaller the further you move to the left of zero:

–5 –4 –3 –2 –1 0 1 2 3 4 5

← numbers get smaller

So, –2 is bigger than –5 and –4 is smaller than –3.

Test yourself

1 Fill in the gaps with the correct word:

smaller or bigger

a) –1 is ________ than 2

b) –7 is ________ than –3

c) –9 is ________ than –15

d) –24 is ________ than –42

2 Write each list of numbers in order (smallest to largest).

a) 8 –6 5 –1 –2 7

b) 9 –7 –10 2 –3 0

3 Write these temperatures in order from coldest to hottest:

–3 °C 15 °C –18 °C 3 °C –11 °C 1 °C

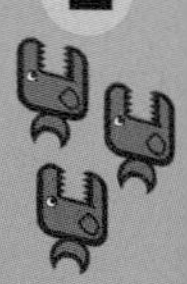

13 Adding and subtracting with negative numbers

Check the facts

When adding and subtracting numbers, it is useful to think of numbers on a line:

–7 –6 –5 –4 –3 –2 –1 0 1 2 3 4 5 6 7

Always count from zero (0).

For **positive** numbers, count to the right of 0.
For **negative** numbers, count to the left of 0.

Example: Calculate: 4 – 7 + 6

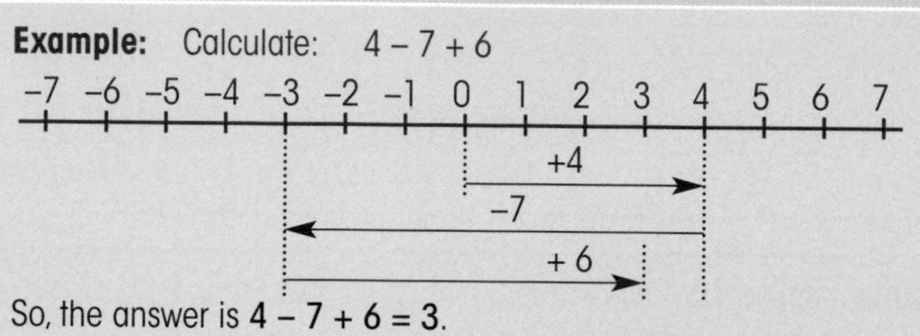

So, the answer is 4 – 7 + 6 = 3.

Sometimes two signs appear together in a calculation.
Two signs can be replaced by one sign using these rules:

+ + gives +	+ – gives –	– + gives –	– – gives +

Example: Calculate: 3 + –5: 3 + –5 = 3 – 5 = –2
–4 – –9: – 4 – –9 = –4 + 9 = 5

Test yourself

1 Calculate:
a) 3 – 7 + 2 b) –1 –5 + 9 c) –4 + 2 –6
d) –2 – –3 e) 10 – –7 f) –1 + –4

2 What do you have to add to:
a) – 5 to get 1? b) –2 to get 5? c) 7 to get –3?

3 Look at these lists of temperatures taken at 11 am and 11 pm on the same day in four British cities.

11 am			
Glasgow	–4 °C	Oxford	5 °C
Leeds	–1 °C	Bristol	6 °C

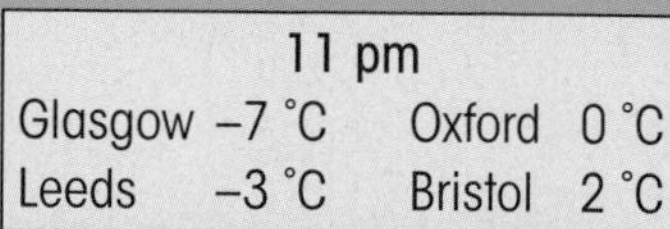

11 pm			
Glasgow	–7 °C	Oxford	0 °C
Leeds	–3 °C	Bristol	2 °C

a) How much warmer is Glasgow at 11 am than 11 pm?
b) How much colder is Leeds than Oxford at 11 am?
c) How much warmer is Bristol at 11 am than Glasgow at 11 pm?

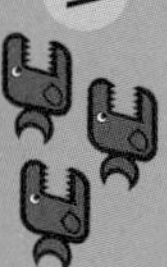

Multiplying and dividing with negative numbers

Check the facts

You already know a **positive** number multiplied/divided by a **positive** number gives a **positive** number:

+ × + = positive number
+ ÷ + = positive number
Examples: 5 × 6 = 30 32 ÷ 8 = 4

What about a positive number multiplied/divided by a negative number?

+ × − = −
+ ÷ − = −
Examples: 2 × −7 = −14 12 ÷ −4 = −3

What about a negative number multiplied/divided by a positive number?

− × + = −
− ÷ + = −
Examples: −5 × 5 = −25 27 ÷ −3 = −9

What about a negative number multiplied/divided by a negative number?

− × − = +
− ÷ − = +
Examples: −8 × −3 = 24 −40 ÷ −10 = 4

You can remember the rule like this:
The **same signs** (+ and + or − and −) give a **positive answer**.
Different signs (+ and − or − and +) give a **negative answer**.

Test yourself

1 Calculate:

a) 4 × −7
b) −1 × 9
c) −20 ÷ −5
d) −2 × 6
e) 10 ÷ −2
f) −9 × −4
g) 36 ÷ −6
h) −18 ÷ −3
i) 8 × −7

2 Two numbers multiplied together make −6.
Added together they make 1. What are the numbers?

3 Two numbers multiplied together make 12.
Added together they make −7. What are the numbers?

4 The square of 4 is 16. The square of another number is 16.
What is that other number?

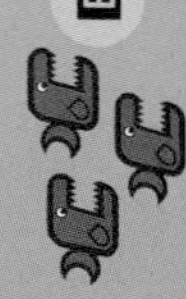

The BODMAS rule

Check the facts

Calculate: $18 \div 3^2 + (5 \times 4)$

Always work out **brackets** first:

$5 \times 4 = 20$, giving $18 \div 3^2 + 20$

Now work out the **order** (power):

$3^2 = 9$, giving $18 \div 9 + 20$

$18 \div 9 + 20 = 2 + 20 =$ **22**

But what if there are no brackets?

Calculate: $18 \div 3^2 + 5 \times 4$

You may reach the following answer:

$18 \div 3^2 = 2$, then $2 + 5 = 7$, then $7 \times 4 =$ **28**

Which is the correct answer: 22 or 28?

There is a rule that will tell us:

Brackets, Order, Divide, Multiply, Add, Subtract

This is called the **BODMAS** rule.

So, to calculate $18 \div 3^2 + 5 \times 4$:

- no **B**rackets
- work out the **O**rder: $3^2 = 9$, giving $18 \div 9 + 5 \times 4$
- then **D**ivide: $18 \div 9 = 2$, giving $2 + 5 \times 4$
- then **M**ultiply: $5 \times 4 = 20$, giving $2 + 20$
- then **A**dd: $2 + 20 = 22$
- no **S**ubtraction.

The answer is 22.

Test yourself

1 Calculate:

a) $3 \times 7 - 6$
b) $8 + 2 \times 5$
c) $10 \div 2 \times 6$
d) $15 \div 3 \times 9$
e) $14 + 7 \div 7$
f) $4 \div 4 - 2$

2 Calculate:

a) $8 \times (9 - 3)$
b) $24 \div (11 - 5)$
c) $(14 + 10) \div 3$
d) $(6 + 4) \times (12 - 5)$

3 Fill in the gaps with the correct maths operation to make each calculation true: + − × ÷

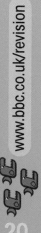

a) 4 ___ 2 ___ 5 = 13
b) 7 ___ 3 ___ 2 = 13
c) (8 ___ 3) ___ 4 = 20
d) (10 ___ 3) ___ 6 = 5

Check the facts

Get to know your calculator!
Some, but not all, calculators use the **BODMAS** rule.

Try this calculation on your calculator: $6 + 8 \div 2 - 3$

- If your calculator uses the **BODMAS** rule, it will:
  Divide first: $8 \div 2 = 4$, giving $6 + 4 - 3$
  then **A**dd: $6 + 4 = 10$, giving $10 - 3$
  then **S**ubtract: $10 - 3 = 7$. The answer is 7.
- If your calculator does not use the **BODMAS** rule, it will:
  Add first: $6 + 8 = 14$, giving $14 \div 2 - 3$
  then **D**ivide: $14 \div 2 = 7$, giving $7 - 3$
  then **S**ubtract: $7 - 3 = 4$. The answer is 4.
- If your calculator uses the BODMAS rule, you can ask it to do the addition first by using brackets:

$$(6 + 8) \div 2 - 3 = 4$$

Also, familiarise yourself with these keys on your calculator:

x^2	square	this key is for squaring a number
$\sqrt{x}$	square root	this key is for finding a square root
x^y y^x	power	this key is for finding powers (to find 2^4 enter 2 x^y 4 =)
+/–	change sign	this key is for entering negative numbers

Test yourself

1 Use your calculator to calculate:
a) $15 - 2 \times 7$, following the BODMAS rule
b) $12 + 18 \div 6$, following the BODMAS rule
c) $18 - 6 \div 2 + 2$, *not* following the BODMAS rule

2 Use your calculator to calculate:
a) 4^5
b) $\sqrt{169}$
c) $-4 + 23$
d) $\sqrt{324}$
e) 18^2
f) $-2 - 14$
g) 7^3
h) $-75 + 15^2$
i) $\sqrt{225} + 5^3$

3 Look at these keys: 9 4 6 3 – ÷ ×
Arrange and enter all these keys so that your calculator gives the answer:
a) 14 b) 3 c) –1

Numbers and calculations

BBC KS3 Check and Test: Maths

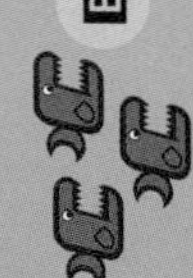

What is a decimal?

Check the facts

A decimal number has a **decimal point** (.).

The decimal point shows where the whole number stops and the decimal fraction begins.

Example: 631.29 (the decimal point shows the whole number is 631 and the decimal fraction is .29)

- You can write decimal numbers in columns:

hundreds	tens	units	.	tenths	hundredths
6	3	1	.	2	9

- You can write decimal numbers as a sum:

6 00 30 1 + $\frac{2}{10}$ + $\frac{9}{100}$

Decimal numbers are used for money. Look at these signs:

COST OF A CALL: only £0.03 per second	The decimal number 0.03 is $\frac{3}{100}$. That is $\frac{3}{100}$ of a pound. That is 3p.
Sale price £37.50	The decimal number is 37.50. That is $30 + 7 + \frac{5}{10} + \frac{0}{100}$.

This number also may be written as 37.5 or 37.500.

- You can put as many or as few zeros as you like on the end of decimal numbers. Zeros on the end of a decimal number do not change its value. They just mean 0 tenths, 0 hundredths, 0 thousandths . . .

Warning! £0.50 ✔ 50p ✔ but £0.50p ✗

You do not know if £0.50p means £0.50 (50p) or 0.5p ($\frac{1}{2}$p).

Test yourself

1 a) How many tenths in the number 4.16?

b) How many hundredths in the number 593.37?

c) How many hundredths in the number 18.205?

d) How many tenths in the number 35.816?

2 Write these sums as decimal numbers:

a) $200 + 70 + 1 + \frac{4}{10} + \frac{0}{100}$

b) $90 + 2 + \frac{3}{10}$

c) $400 + 8 + \frac{6}{100}$

d) $\frac{1}{10} + \frac{9}{100}$

3 Write these money amounts:

a) Four pounds and thirty pence.

b) Fifty-one pounds and nine pence.

c) 8p as a decimal number of £1.

Check the facts

Which of these two decimal numbers is bigger:

4.27 (four point two seven *not* four point twenty-seven) or **4.6** (four point six)?

> When comparing decimal numbers, always begin by:
> - **comparing whole numbers**:
>   4.27 and 4.6 both have the whole number 4.
> - **comparing tenths**:
>   4.27 has 2 tenths, 4.6 has 6 tenths.

4.6 has more tenths, so 4.6 is bigger than 4.27.

You can check this on a number line:

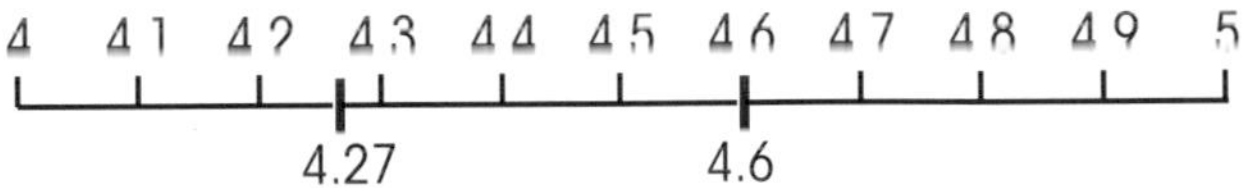

Notice on the number line that 5, not 4.10, comes after 4.9.
(4.10 has no hundredths, so it is in fact the same as 4.1.)

Example: Which is bigger: 75.351 or 75.329?

> Comparing **whole numbers**:
> 75.351 and 75.329 both have whole number 75.
>
> Comparing **tenths**:
> 75.351 and 75.329 both have 3 tenths.
>
> Comparing **hundredths**:
> 75.351 has 5 hundredths, 75.329 has 2 hundredths.
>
> 75.351 has more hundredths. 75.351 is bigger than 75.329.

Test yourself

1 Fill in the gaps with the correct word:

smaller or bigger

a) 10.45 is ____________ than 10.7
b) 234.09 is ____________ than 234.90
c) 0.06 is ____________ than 0.008
d) 7.540 is ____________ than 7.9

2 Write each list of numbers in order, from smallest to largest:

a) 4.05, 4.005, 4.1
b) 0.09, 0.8, 0.62
c) 7.78, 7.779, 7.77
d) 63.4, 6.34, 0.63
e) 91.56, 91.6, 91.5
f) 309.2, 309.02, 309.21
g) 5.67, 5.9, 5.108
h) 23.61, 32.16, 23.6611

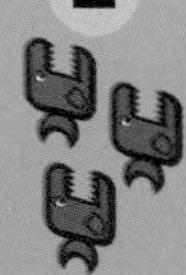

Rounding decimals

Check the facts

A decimal number can be written to one, two, three or more decimal places. The number of decimal places is the number of digits after the decimal point.

> **Example:** **5.58** has two digits after the decimal point.
> So, 5.58 is written to 2 decimal places, or 2.d.p.

7.12 has 2.d.p., but you may want to round it to 1.d.p.

7.0 7.1 7.2 7.3

7.12

7.15

7.12 lies between 7.1 and 7.2.
7.12 is closer to 7.1 than 7.2.
7.12 is rounded off to 7.1 (1.d.p.).

7.15 lies exactly halfway between 7.1 and 7.2.
Numbers that end in 5 are always rounded up.
7.15 is rounded up to 7.2 (1.d.p.).

You may not always want to draw number lines to round decimal numbers. Instead, round a decimal number by drawing a line where the rounded number will end.

> **If the number after the line is 4 or less, round off.**
> **If the number after the line is 5 or more, round up.**

Examples:

If rounding 4.569 to 2.d.p., the number will end at 4.56|9.
The number after the line is 9, so **round up** to 4.57 (2.d.p.).
If rounding 0.8346 to 1.d.p., the number will end at 0.8|346.
The number after the line is 3, so **round off** to 0.8 (1.d.p.).

Test yourself

1 Round each of the following decimal numbers to 1.d.p.

a) 8.93　c) 0.555　e) 92.451　g) 0.6715
b) 62.78　d) 35.81　f) 107.67　h) 241.719

2 Round each of the following decimal numbers to 2.d.p.

a) 67.9281　c) 0.0251　e) 19.1920
b) 4.501　d) 82.1144　f) 1.299

3 Round each of the following decimal numbers to 3.d.p.

a) 5829.2486　c) 3.141593　e) 9.2769
b) 0.2083　d) 29.48129　f) 2.3999

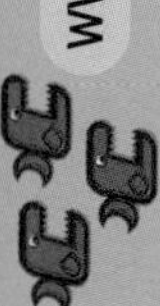

Adding and subtracting decimals

Check the facts

Add and subtract decimals in the same way that you add and subtract whole numbers. Line up digits so that hundreds, tens, units, tenths, hundredths . . . each have their own column. If you have done this correctly, the decimal points should be in line too.

Example: Calculate: 42.32 + 0.88

```
   42.32
+   0.88
   43.20
    1 1
```

Sometimes, when adding and subtracting decimals, you may wish to insert zero(s) at the end of a decimal to help you with your calculation:

Example: Calculate: 65.7 – 4.41

```
   65.6/7 1 0
–   4.41
   61.29
```

Sometimes, when adding or subtracting a decimal and a whole number, you may wish to insert a **decimal point** to help you with your calculation:

Example: Calculate: 68 + 3.44

```
   68.00
+   3.44
   71.44
   1
```

Test yourself

1 Calculate using pen and paper (not forgetting to show your working):

a) 4.67 + 23.9 d) 51.78 +102 g) 309.6 – 7.98
b) 89.1 – 32.7 e) 20.99 + 0.01 h) 192 – 55.13
c) 32.82 – 5.7 f) 41.9 – 0.17 i) 510 – 6.89

2 What is the total cost of the items on each of these receipts?

receipt (a)	**receipt** (b)	**receipt** (c)	**receipt** (d)
£6.99	£7.33	£0.89	£13.77
£19.50	£23.55	£0.45	£22.08
£0.55	£4.17	£1.75	£3.99
£1.09	£1.99	£3.95	£98

Multiplying and dividing decimals by single-digit whole numbers

Check the facts

Multiply and divide decimals by single-digit whole numbers in the same way that you multiply and divide whole numbers. The decimal point in the calculation should line up with the decimal point in the answer.

Example: Calculate: 61.25 × 7

$$\begin{array}{r} 61.25 \\ \times \quad 7 \\ \hline 428.75 \\ \hline {}^{1\ \ 3} \end{array}$$

Look! 5 × 7 = 35. Carry the 3.
2 × 7 = 14, add the 3, makes 17. Carry the 1.
1 × 7 = 7, add the 1, makes 8.
6 × 7 = 42. **Answer:** 428.75

Example: Calculate: 93.4 ÷ 4

$$\begin{array}{r} 23.35 \\ 4 \overline{)\, 9\,{}^{1}3\,.\,{}^{1}4\,{}^{2}0} \end{array}$$

Look! 9 ÷ 4 = 2 remainder 1. Carry the 1.
13 ÷ 4 = 3 remainder 1. Carry the 1.
14 ÷ 4 = 3 remainder 2. Carry the 2.
Insert a zero to help with the calculation.
20 ÷ 4 = 5 **Answer:** 23.35

Remember! Zeros on the end of a decimal number do not change the value of the number.

Test yourself

1 Calculate (showing all your working):

a) 7.61 × 8	d) 51.44 ÷ 4	g) 52.9 × 2
b) 81.32 × 5	e) 0.62 × 9	h) 1446.96 ÷ 6
c) 7.14 ÷ 3	f) 453.46 ÷ 7	i) 522.91 × 8

Did you get any answers wrong? To get more practice, make up calculations of your own and check the answers on a calculator.

2

DAISY CAKES
Large birthday cakes: £14.25 Small birthday cakes: £

a) Six large birthday cakes were ordered this week. How much money is that altogether? Show your working.

b) The Daisy Cakes sign has been torn.
Eight small birthday cakes were ordered this week.
Altogether they came to £67.60. How much is each small birthday cake? Show your working.

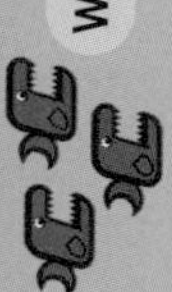

Check the facts

Multiply decimal numbers by 10 by moving each digit one place to the left:

	hundreds	tens	units	.	tenths	hundredths
		3	2	.	7	1
32.71 × 10	3	2	7	.	1	

Examples: 9.6 × 10 = 96 63.106 × 10 = 631.06

Multiply decimal numbers by 100 by moving each digit two places to the left:

	hundreds	tens	units	.	tenths	hundredths
			5	.	9	
5.9 × 100	5	9	0			

Examples: 4.31 × 100 = 431 0.6 × 100 = 60

Divide decimal numbers by 10 by moving each digit one place to the right:

	hundreds	tens	units	.	tenths	hundredths
		7	3	.	8	
73.8 ÷ 10			7	.	3	8

Examples: 5.3 ÷ 10 = 0.53 0.99 ÷ 10 = 0.099

Divide decimal numbers by 100 by moving each digit two places to the right:

	hundreds	tens	units	.	tenths	h'dths	th'ths
		4	6	.	1		
46.1 ÷ 100			0	.	4	6	1

Examples: 9.2 ÷ 100 = 0.092 24.19 ÷ 100 = 0.2419

Test yourself

1 Calculate

a) 4.67 ÷ 10
b) 56.1 × 10
c) 77.8 × 100
d) 60.81 ÷ 100
e) 3.4 ÷ 100
f) 0.7 × 100

2 Fill in the gaps with the correct number: 10 or 100.

a) 9.37 ÷ ______ = 0.0937
b) 0.01 × ______ = 1
c) 46.8 ÷ ______ = 0.468
d) 5.691 × ______ = 56.91
e) 8.961 × ______ = 896.1
f) 70.06 ÷ ______ = 7.006

Did you get any answers wrong? To get more practice, make up calculations of your own and check the answers on a calculator.

What is a fraction?

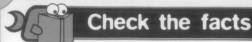

Check the facts

A fraction is a part of a whole. A fraction is written as:

$$\frac{\textbf{numerator (top number)}}{\textbf{denominator (bottom number)}}$$

The **denominator** is the number of equal parts in the whole.
The **numerator** is the number of equal parts in the fraction.

This rectangle is **one whole**:

The rectangle is split into **nine equal parts**:

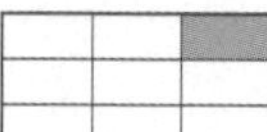

If any one part is shaded,
then $\frac{1}{9}$ is shaded and $\frac{8}{9}$ is not shaded:

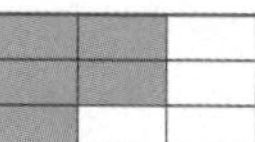

If any five parts are shaded,
then $\frac{5}{9}$ is shaded and $\frac{4}{9}$ is not shaded:

If nine parts are shaded,
then $\frac{9}{9}$ is shaded. That's a whole, or 1.

Any fraction with a denominator equal to its numerator is equal to 1
(so, $\frac{13}{13} = 1$, $\frac{4}{4} = 1$, $\frac{26}{26} = 1$, $\frac{501}{501} = 1$).

Test yourself

1 Look at the diagrams below. In each diagram, what fraction is shaded? What fraction is not shaded?

a)  b) 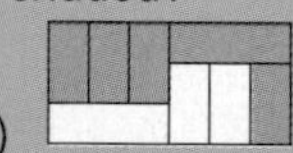 c) 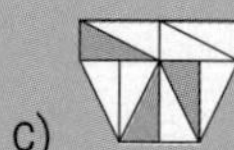

2 Draw four squares.

a) Divide your first square into the correct number of equal parts to shade the fraction $\frac{1}{2}$.

b) Divide your second square into the correct number of equal parts to shade the fraction $\frac{3}{4}$.

c) Divide your third square into the correct number of equal parts to shade the fraction $\frac{7}{8}$.

d) Divide your fourth square into the correct number of equal parts and shade to show the fraction $\frac{5}{12}$.

Check the facts

This rectangle is split into three equal parts.
$\frac{2}{3}$ is shaded and $\frac{1}{3}$ is not shaded.

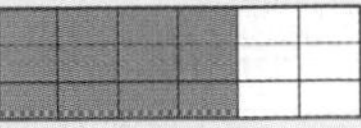

This rectangle is split into nine equal parts.
$\frac{6}{9}$ is shaded and $\frac{3}{9}$ is not shaded.

This rectangle is split into 18 equal parts.
$\frac{12}{18}$ is shaded and $\frac{6}{18}$ is not shaded.

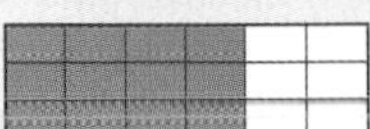

Notice, the same area is shaded in each rectangle.
So, $\frac{2}{3} = \frac{6}{9} = \frac{12}{18}$. These are **equivalent fractions**.

The **numerator** and **denominator** of $\frac{2}{3}$ have been multiplied:

- by 3 to make $\frac{6}{9}$: $\frac{2 \times 3}{3 \times 3} = \frac{6}{9}$
- by 6 to make $\frac{12}{18}$: $\frac{2 \times 6}{3 \times 6} = \frac{12}{18}$

If you multiply or divide the top and bottom of a fraction by the same number, its value does not change. When dividing, this is called cancelling down or writing a fraction in its lowest terms.

Examples: $\frac{2}{3} = \frac{2 \times 2}{3 \times 2} = \frac{4}{6}$ so, $\frac{2}{3} = \frac{4}{6}$

$\frac{9}{12} = \frac{9 \div 3}{12 \div 3} = \frac{3}{4}$ so, $\frac{9}{12} = \frac{3}{4}$

($\frac{9}{12}$ cancels down to $\frac{3}{4}$)

Test yourself

1 Write these fractions as twentieths, $\frac{}{20}$:

a) $\frac{1}{5}$ b) $\frac{1}{4}$ c) $\frac{1}{10}$ d) $\frac{3}{4}$ e) $\frac{7}{10}$

2 Write these fractions as twenty-fourths, $\frac{}{24}$:

a) $\frac{7}{12}$ b) $\frac{2}{3}$ c) $\frac{5}{6}$ d) $\frac{3}{4}$ e) $\frac{1}{2}$

3 Fill in the missing denominator or numerator:

a) $\frac{?}{9} = \frac{6}{27}$ b) $\frac{12}{30} = \frac{2}{?}$ c) $\frac{6}{8} = \frac{?}{16}$

4 Look at these six fraction cards:

A 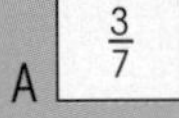 $\frac{3}{7}$ B  C 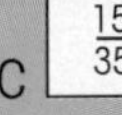 $\frac{15}{35}$ D 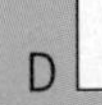 $\frac{15}{24}$ E 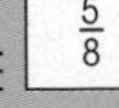 $\frac{5}{8}$ F 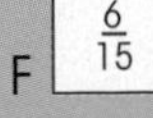 $\frac{6}{15}$

There are three pairs of equivalent fractions. Find the pairs.

Ordering fractions

Check the facts

Order fractions by finding equivalent fractions with the same denominator. This is called finding a common denominator.

Example: Write these fractions in order, from smallest to largest:

$\frac{3}{4}$ $\frac{2}{3}$ $\frac{5}{6}$

$\frac{3}{4}, \frac{2}{3}, \frac{5}{6}$ have equivalent fractions with denominator 12 ($\frac{}{4}, \frac{}{3}, \frac{}{6}$ can all be multiplied to make $\frac{}{12}$, a common denominator of 12, because 4, 3 and 6 all divide into 12):

$$\frac{3}{4} = \frac{3 \times 3}{4 \times 3} = \frac{9}{12}, \qquad \frac{2}{3} = \frac{2 \times 4}{3 \times 4} = \frac{8}{12}, \qquad \frac{5}{6} = \frac{5 \times 2}{6 \times 2} = \frac{10}{12}$$

The fractions in size order, from smallest to largest, are:

$\frac{8}{12}, \frac{9}{12}, \frac{10}{12}$, that is $\frac{2}{3}, \frac{3}{4}, \frac{5}{6}$.

Test yourself

1 Write each list of fractions in order, from smallest to largest:

a) $\frac{5}{6}, \frac{1}{2}, \frac{1}{3}$ c) $\frac{2}{6}, \frac{3}{8}, \frac{5}{24}, \frac{1}{4}$ e) $\frac{2}{5}, \frac{1}{2}, \frac{7}{10}$

b) $\frac{3}{5}, \frac{11}{15}, \frac{2}{3}$ d) $\frac{13}{20}, \frac{7}{10}, \frac{2}{5}, \frac{1}{4}$ f) $\frac{7}{9}, \frac{5}{6}, \frac{3}{4}$.

2 Look at these fraction cards:

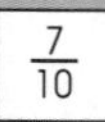
$\frac{7}{10}$ $\frac{3}{5}$ $\frac{1}{3}$ $\frac{5}{6}$
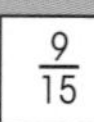
$\frac{9}{15}$

a) Caroline takes the card showing the smallest fraction. Which card does she take?

b) Mark takes the card showing the largest fraction. Which card does he take?

c) Amy takes the card that can be shaded as: 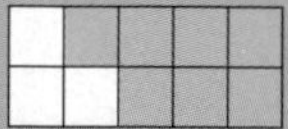

d) Jeannie takes the two remaining cards.

Jeannie says they show equivalent fractions. Is Jeannie right?

Check the facts

You can only add and subtract fractions with the same denominator **(common denominator)**. Fifths can only be added to or subtracted from fifths. Ninths can only be added to or subtracted from ninths, and so on.

Add and subtract fractions of the same denominator like this:

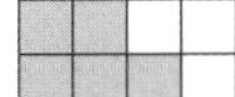

$\frac{5}{8} + \frac{1}{8} = \frac{6}{8}$

$\frac{7}{9} - \frac{2}{9} = \frac{5}{9}$

Add and subtract fractions of different denominators by finding equivalent fractions with the same denominator. This is called finding a **common denominator**.

Example: Calculate: $\frac{7}{15} + \frac{2}{5}$

$\frac{2}{5}$ has an equivalent fraction with denominator 15.
The common denominator is 15: $\frac{2}{5} = \frac{2 \times 3}{5 \times 3} = \frac{6}{15}$
So, $\frac{7}{15} + \frac{2}{5} = \frac{7}{15} + \frac{6}{15} = \frac{13}{15}$

Example: Calculate: $\frac{1}{2} - \frac{3}{7}$

$\frac{1}{2}$ and $\frac{3}{7}$ have equivalent fractions with denominator 14.
The common denominator is 14: $\frac{1}{2} = \frac{1 \times 7}{2 \times 7} = \frac{7}{14}$
$\frac{3}{7} = \frac{3 \times 2}{7 \times 2} = \frac{6}{14}$
So, $\frac{1}{2} - \frac{3}{7} = \frac{7}{14} - \frac{6}{14} = \frac{1}{14}$

Test yourself

1 Calculate:

a) $\frac{7}{11} - \frac{2}{11}$ c) $\frac{1}{5} + \frac{2}{3}$ e) $\frac{2}{3} - \frac{4}{9}$

b) $\frac{4}{5} - \frac{3}{10}$ d) $\frac{3}{8} + \frac{1}{6}$ f) $\frac{5}{6} + \frac{1}{10}$

2 Jon mixes blue and red paints to make purple paint. $\frac{5}{8}$ of Jon's purple paint mixture is blue paint. What fraction of Jon's purple paint mixture is red paint?

3 Antony makes a fruit drink. $\frac{1}{2}$ the drink is grapefruit juice. $\frac{1}{5}$ of the drink is cranberry juice. The rest of the drink is orange juice. What fraction of the drink is orange juice?

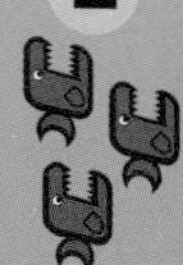

Mixed numbers, improper fractions and reciprocals

Check the facts

Mixed numbers have a whole number part and a fractional part.

Examples: $4\frac{12}{13}$, $29\frac{4}{35}$, $735\frac{23}{48}$

Improper fractions have a numerator bigger than their denominator.

Examples: $\frac{8}{7}$, $\frac{31}{15}$, $\frac{55}{2}$

Remember: any fraction with a denominator equal to its numerator is equal to 1 (e.g. $\frac{5}{5} = 1$).

Convert **mixed numbers** to improper fractions like this:

$2\frac{3}{5} = \frac{5}{5} + \frac{5}{5} + \frac{3}{5} = \frac{13}{5}$

Or, the quick way is to work out $2 \times 5 + 3 = 13$, giving $\frac{13}{5}$.

When adding or subtracting mixed numbers, add or subtract the whole numbers first, then add or subtract the fractions.

Example: $2\frac{3}{5} + 5\frac{1}{3} = 2 + 5 + \frac{3}{5} + \frac{1}{3}$

$= 2 + 5 + \frac{9}{15} + \frac{5}{15} = 7\frac{14}{15}$

Convert **improper fractions** to mixed numbers like this:

$\frac{9}{2} = \frac{2}{2} + \frac{2}{2} + \frac{2}{2} + \frac{2}{2} + \frac{1}{2} = 4\frac{1}{2}$

Or, the quick way is to work out $9 \div 2 = 4$ remainder 1, giving $4\frac{1}{2}$.

The **reciprocal** of a fraction is the fraction turned upside-down.

Example: The reciprocal of $\frac{15}{26}$ is $\frac{26}{15}$.

Test yourself

1 Convert these mixed numbers to improper fractions:

a) $3\frac{4}{5}$ b) $9\frac{1}{2}$ c) $7\frac{2}{3}$ d) $10\frac{3}{8}$

2 Convert these improper fractions to mixed numbers:

a) $\frac{14}{5}$ b) $\frac{11}{3}$ c) $\frac{32}{9}$ d) $\frac{27}{4}$

3 Calculate:

a) $4\frac{3}{5} + 9\frac{1}{5}$ c) $10\frac{5}{7} - 6\frac{1}{7}$ e) $7\frac{9}{10} - 2\frac{1}{5}$

b) $8\frac{5}{11} - 3\frac{1}{11}$ d) $9\frac{1}{3} - 8\frac{1}{6}$ f) $9\frac{1}{4} + 11\frac{1}{3}$

4 Find the reciprocal of each of these fractions:

a) $\frac{7}{11}$ b) $\frac{2}{34}$ c) $\frac{3}{4}$ d) $\frac{5}{8}$

Multiplying and dividing fractions

Check the facts

Multiply fractions by multiplying the numerators and the denominators.

Example: $\frac{1}{2} \times \frac{4}{5} = \frac{1 \times 4}{2 \times 5} = \frac{4}{10}$ (= $\frac{2}{5}$ cancelled down)

Divide fractions by multiplying the first fraction by the reciprocal of the second fraction. (**Remember:** the reciprocal of a fraction is the fraction turned upside-down.)

Example: $\frac{5}{8} \div \frac{1}{4} = \frac{5}{8} \times \frac{4}{1} = \frac{5 \times 4}{8 \times 1} = \frac{20}{8} = 2\,\frac{4}{8} = 2\,\frac{1}{2}$

Multiply or divide mixed numbers by converting them to improper fractions.

Example:

$8\,\frac{2}{5} \div \frac{1}{10} = \frac{42}{5} \div \frac{1}{10} = \frac{42}{5} \times \frac{10}{1} = \frac{42 \times 10}{5 \times 1} = \frac{420}{5} = 84$

Calculate fractions on your calculator using the key: $a\frac{b}{c}$

Try this example on your calculator: $3\,\frac{4}{15} \times \frac{2}{7} =$

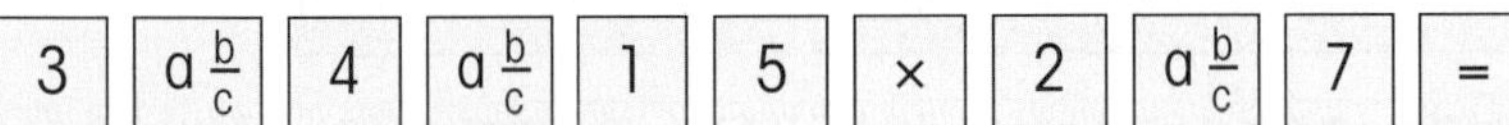

Did you get the answer $\frac{14}{15}$?

Test yourself

1 Calculate without a calculator:

a) $\frac{3}{4} \times \frac{1}{5}$ c) $\frac{2}{7} \times \frac{2}{3}$ e) $\frac{1}{6} \div \frac{3}{8}$

b) $\frac{7}{9} \times \frac{2}{9}$ d) $\frac{3}{10} \div \frac{4}{7}$ f) $\frac{2}{5} \div \frac{9}{10}$

2 Calculate with a calculator:

a) $\frac{4}{11} \div \frac{12}{13}$ b) $\frac{9}{25} \times \frac{5}{8}$ c) $\frac{11}{20} \div \frac{3}{5}$

3 Look at these calculator buttons:

1	2	3	5	$a\frac{b}{c}$	$a\frac{b}{c}$	÷	=

Arrange the buttons in the correct order to get the following answers:

a) $\frac{5}{6}$ b) $1\frac{1}{5}$ c) $3\,\frac{1}{3}$ d) $7\frac{1}{2}$

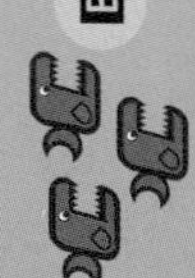

Calculating fractions of whole numbers

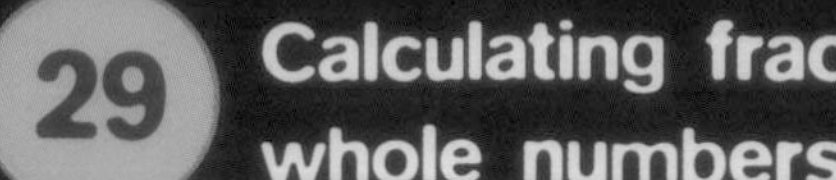

Check the facts

Finding $\frac{1}{2}$ of a whole is the same as dividing a whole by 2.

$\frac{1}{2}$ of ◯ = ◖   ◯ ÷ 2 = ◖

Finding $\frac{1}{3}$ of a whole is the same as dividing a whole by 3.

$\frac{1}{3}$ of ▯▯▯ = ▯   ▯▯▯ ÷ 3 = ▯

Find fractions of whole numbers by

- calculating **one part** of the fraction using **division**
- calculating **more parts** of the fraction using **multiplication**.

Example:

Find $\frac{3}{5}$ of 35:

calculate 1 part of the fraction, $\frac{1}{5}$:   35 ÷ 5 = 7

calculate 3 lots of $\frac{1}{5}$ to find $\frac{3}{5}$:   3 × 7 = 21

so, $\frac{3}{5}$ of 35 = 21

In mathematics, 'of' means multiply, so you can calculate $\frac{1}{4}$ of 68 on your calculator by punching in $\frac{1}{4}$ × 68.

That is: 1 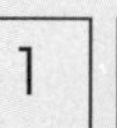 4 × 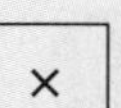 8 

Did you get the answer 17?

Test yourself

1 Calculate:

a) $\frac{1}{4}$ of 36 litres   c) $\frac{4}{7}$ of £56   e) $\frac{3}{10}$ of £4.50

b) $\frac{2}{5}$ of 30 grams   d) $\frac{5}{6}$ of 24 hours   f) $\frac{5}{9}$ of £27

2 There are 32 houses in the street where Geraldine lives.

$\frac{5}{8}$ of the houses have three bedrooms.

$\frac{3}{8}$ of the houses have four bedrooms.

a) How many three-bedroom houses are there in Geraldine's street?

b) How many four-bedroom houses are there in Geraldine's street?

Check the facts

Per cent (%) means 'in every hundred'.

The whole is 100%, meaning '100 in every hundred'.

Percentages can be written as a fraction with a denominator of 100.

Examples: $4\% = \frac{4}{100}$ $56\% = \frac{56}{100}$

Percentages can also be expressed as a decimal by dividing by 100.

Examples: $4\% = 4 \div 100 = 0.04$ $56\% = 56 \div 100 = 0.56$

Here are some common percentages that you should know:

$75\% = \frac{75}{100}$ (cancels down to $\frac{3}{4}$) $75\% = 75 \div 100 = 0.75$

$50\% = \frac{50}{100}$ (cancels down to $\frac{1}{2}$) $50\% = 50 \div 100 = 0.5$

$25\% = \frac{25}{100}$ (cancels down to $\frac{1}{4}$) $25\% = 25 \div 100 = 0.25$

$10\% = \frac{10}{100}$ (cancels down to $\frac{1}{10}$) $10\% = 10 \div 100 = 0.1$

Percentages, fractions and decimals are all linked. Look at these examples:

$25\% + 50\% = 75\%$

$\frac{25}{100} + \frac{50}{100} = \frac{75}{100}$

$0.25 + 0.5 = 0.75$

$75\% + 25\% = 100\%$

$\frac{75}{100} + \frac{25}{100} = \frac{100}{100} = 1$

$0.75 + 0.25 = 1$

Test yourself

1 Write each of these percentages as fractions in their lowest terms (cancelled down) and then as decimals:

a) 10% c) 75% e) 5% g) 8%
b) 25% d) 30% f) 70% h) 15%

2 Look at these eight sales tags:

A: SAVE 60% SAVE SAVE

C: SAVE 10%

E: ALL $\frac{1}{2}$ PRICE

G: 20% SALE

B: Everything $\frac{1}{5}$ off

D: 

F: A SAVING OF 50%!

H: 

There are four pairs of tags that show the same discount. Find the pairs.

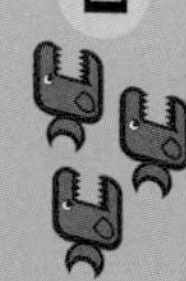

Calculating percentages

Check the facts

Find percentages that are multiples of 10 by finding 10% and then multiplying.

Example: Calculate: 70% of 60 g

10% of 60 g = $\frac{1}{10}$ of 60 g = 6 g

70% of 60 g = 10% of 60 g × 7 = 6 g × 7 = 42 g

Use 10% to find percentages that end in 5.

Example: Calculate: 45% of £80

10% of £80 = $\frac{1}{10}$ of £80 = £8

5% of £80 = 10% of £80 ÷ 2 = £8 ÷ 2 = £4

40% of £80 = 10% of £80 × 4 = £8 × 4 = £32

45% of £80 = 5% of £80 + 40% of £80 = £4 + £32 = £36

Find more difficult percentages by multiplying the percentage as a fraction or a decimal by the quantity.

Examples:

18% of 42 kg = $\frac{18}{100}$ × 42 = (18 × 42) ÷ 100 = 7.56 kg

or 18% of 42 kg = 0.18 × 42 = 7.56 kg

57% of £35 = $\frac{57}{100}$ × 35 = (57 × 35) ÷ 100 = £19.95

or 57% of £35 = 0.57 × 35 = £19.95

Test yourself

1 Calculate these percentages, showing your working:

a) 30% of 20 hours
b) 80% of 50 cm
c) 15% of 60 kg
d) 95% of \$40
e) 45% of £30
f) 75% of 32 minutes

2 Calculate these percentages, using your calculator:

a) 12% of £38
b) 9% of 125 km
c) 26% of 85 g
d) 99% of £420

3 Four hundred students attend Thrupp School. On 13 December:

- 2% of students were absent due to illness
- 1.5% of students were absent due to bad weather.

a) How many students were absent due to illness?
b) How many students were absent due to bad weather?

Expressing a number as a percentage of another number

Check the facts

Use percentages to make comparisons.

Example:
AF Computers are offering sale prices on 81 of their 300 computers.
BN Computers are offering sale prices on 112 of their 350 computers.

You can use percentages to compare the sales and work out who has the biggest sale stock.

Express one number as a percentage of another by writing the first number as a fraction of the second number and then multiplying the fraction by 100 to make a percentage.

Example: Express sale stock as a percentage of all stock:

AF Computers have $\frac{81}{300} \times 100 = 27\%$ sale stock
BN Computers have $\frac{112}{350} \times 100 = 32\%$ sale stock

Therefore, BN Computers has the most sale stock.

Test yourself

You may use your calculator to answer the following questions.

1 There are 400 animals at Osney Zoo. 56 are reptiles.
There are 250 animals at Norham Zoo. 45 are reptiles.
Which zoo has the bigger proportion of reptiles?

2 There are 32 students in Mrs Alter's class. 14 are boys.
There are 30 students in Mrs Scott's class. 12 are boys.
Whose class has the bigger proportion of boys?

3 Bridge Park was visited today by 80 people. 28 walk dogs.
Rock Park was visited today by 125 people. 55 walk dogs.
East Park was visited today by 96 people. 36 walk dogs.
a) Which park had the biggest proportion of dog-walkers?
b) Which park had the smallest proportion?

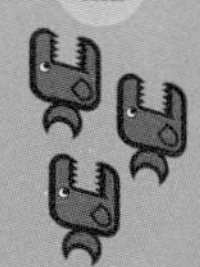

33 Converting between fractions, decimals and percentages

Check the facts

Change decimals to fractions by looking at place value.
Examples: $0.9 = \frac{9}{10}$, $0.44 = \frac{44}{100} = \frac{11}{25}$ (cancelled down)

Change fractions to decimals by dividing numerator by denominator.
Examples: $\frac{3}{8} = 3 \div 8 = 0.375$, $\frac{24}{25} = 0.96$

> $\frac{1}{3}$ as a decimal is $1 \div 3 = 0.33333\ldots$ the 3 repeats for ever. This is a recurring decimal and is written as $\mathbf{0.\dot{3}}$.
>
> A dot is written above the number or numbers that repeat.
>
> Examples: $\frac{7}{9} = 0.\dot{7}$, $\frac{1}{6} = 0.1\dot{6}$

Change decimals to percentages by multiplying by 100.
Examples: $0.07 \times 100 = 7$, so $0.07 = 7\%$, $0.68 = 68\%$

Change fractions to percentages by multiplying by 100.
Examples: $\frac{9}{20} \times 100 = 45$, so $\frac{9}{20} = 45\%$, $\frac{61}{305} = 20\%$

Change percentages to decimals by dividing by 100.
Examples: $5\% = 5 \div 100 = 0.05$, $23\% = 0.23$

Change percentages to fractions by writing 100 as a denominator.
Examples: $41\% = \frac{41}{100}$, $8\% = \frac{8}{100} = \frac{2}{25}$ (cancelled down)

Test yourself

1 Convert these decimals to fractions and percentages:
a) 0.21 b) 0.53 c) 0.79 d) 0.06

2 Convert these fractions to decimals and percentages:
a) $\frac{11}{50}$ b) $\frac{7}{10}$ c) $\frac{23}{25}$ d) $\frac{57}{75}$

3 Convert these percentages to fractions (cancelled down to their lowest terms) and decimals:
a) 2% b) 32% c) 72% d) 55%

4 Look at these eight numbers:

A	C	E	G
35%	60%	0.36	0.6

B	D	F	H
$\frac{3}{10}$	$\frac{9}{25}$	$\frac{7}{20}$	30%

Find the pairs of cards that show equivalent decimals, fractions or percentages.

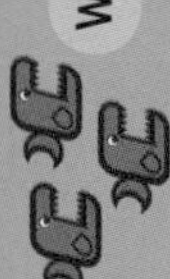

Rounding to the nearest whole number, 10 or 100

Check the facts

Round a decimal number to the **nearest whole number** by:

- **rounding up** if the decimal part is 0.5 or more
- **rounding down** if the decimal part is less that 0.5.

Examples:

26.8 has a decimal part of 0.8. Round **up** 26.8 to 27.

31.29 has a decimal part of 0.29. Round **down** 31.29 to 31.

You can see that 26.8 is closer to 27 than 26 and 31.29 is closer to 31 than 32:

25 26 27 28 29 30 31 32

26.8 31.29

Round a number to the **nearest 10** by:

- **rounding up** if the number has 5 or more units
- **rounding down** if the number has less than 5 units.

Examples: 83 has 3 units. Round **down** 83 to 80.

107 has 7 units. Round **up** 107 to 110.

Round a number to the **nearest 100** by:

- **rounding up** if the number has 5 or more tens
- **rounding down** if the number has less than 5 tens.

Examples: 654 has 5 tens. Round **up** 654 to 700.

347 has 4 tens. Round **down** 347 to 300.

Test yourself

1 Round each of these decimal numbers to the nearest whole number:

a) 56.7 b) 13.19 c) 3.7 d) 433.29

2 Round each of these numbers to the nearest 10:

a) 32 b) 66 c) 381 d) 44.5

3 A jar of 2 pences contains £60 (to the nearest £10).
Which of these amounts could be in this jar?

£52 £56.20 £63.12 £51.70 £55 £68.18

4 Round each of these numbers to the nearest 100:

a) 778 b) 300.2 c) 3781 d) 64

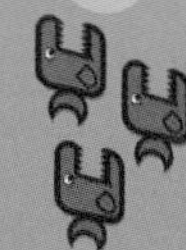

Approximating answers to calculations

Check the facts

Approximate answers to calculations by rounding each number in the calculation. As a guide:

- round decimals 1 to 10 to the **nearest whole number**
- round any number with a two-figure whole number to the **nearest 10**
- round any number with a three-figure whole number to the **nearest 100.**

Example: Ross calculates $\frac{82 \times 4.9}{189.7}$ on a calculator.

Ross gets the answer 2.12. Could this be correct?

82 is a two-figure whole number.
82 is approximately 80 (nearest 10).
4.9 is a decimal number between 1 and 10.
4.9 is approximately 5 (nearest whole number).
189.7 is a number with a three-figure whole number.
189.7 is approximately 200 (nearest 100).
So, $\frac{82 \times 4.9}{189.7}$ is approximately $\frac{80 \times 5}{200} = \frac{400}{200} = 400 \div 200 = 2$
And 2 is close to 2.12. *Ross could be correct.*

When shopping, it can be useful to approximate the bill.

Example: Wrapping paper is £1.99 a roll. I want to buy four rolls. Approximately how much will this cost?

£1.99 is approximately £2. So, four rolls = 4 × £2 = £8.

Test yourself

1 Approximate answers to the following calculations:

a) $31.9 \div 6.2$ d) 9.12×42 g) $(58 + 41) \div 19$
b) 1.85×211 e) $(1.8 - 0.9) \times 51$ h) $(123 - 54.99) \times 3.5$
c) $777 \div 4.29$ f) $(9.8 + 10.15) \div 5.2$

2 CDs are on sale at £5.99 each. Ginny has a £30-gift voucher. How many CDs can she buy with her voucher?

3 Chocolate bars are being sold in packs of three for 99p. How many bars can Carolyn buy with a £5 note?

Understanding unitary method

Check the facts

If you know a quantity such as the weight, length or cost of several items, you can use **division** to find the weight, length or cost of one item.

Examples:

- Russell buys 24 boiled sweets. In total they weigh 30 g. How much does one boiled sweet weigh?

24 sweets weigh 30 g.	So, 1 sweet weighs 24 ÷ 30 = 0.8 g.

- Stuart buys 6 tins of paint to paint his kitchen. The total cost of the paint is £54.60. How much is each tin of paint?

6 tins cost £54.60.	So, 1 tin costs £54.60 ÷ 6 = £9.10.

Once you have calculated the weight, length or cost of one item (the unit), use **multiplication** to find the weight, length or cost of any number of items.

Example:

- Colin buys 4 shirts and pays a total of £62. Dan buys 3 of the same shirts as Colin. How much does Dan pay in total?

4 shirts cost £62.	So, 1 shirt costs £62 ÷ 4 = £15.50.
1 shirt costs £15.50.	So, 3 shirts cost £15.50 × 3 = £45.45.

Test yourself

1 Eight cups fit exactly on a shelf of length 72 cm.

a) How wide is each cup?

b) How long would the shelf be if it holds 10 cups?

2 A crisp factory packs packets of crisps into boxes. The same number of packets are packed in each box.

a) A newsagent receives 100 packets of crisps in 5 boxes.
How many packets of crisps are in each box?

b) A supermarket has 40 boxes of crisps delivered.
How many packets of crisps are in all 40 boxes?

3 Stan buys 5 bottles of lemonade and pays £5.50 in total.
Geraldine buys 7 bottles of the same lemonade. How much does Geraldine pay?

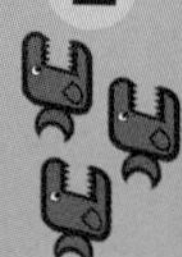

What is a ratio?

Check the facts

Ratios are a way of comparing quantities.
Ratios are written as one number : another number

Example: The ratio of pens to pencils in Kamal's pencil case is 3 : 4.
That means for every 3 pens there are 4 pencils.

> Warning! Change the order and it means something else:
> **4 : 3** means for every 4 pens there are 3 pencils.

- If for every 3 pens, there are 4 pencils,
  6 pens means 8 pencils and 9 pens means 12 pencils.

> 3 : 4, 6 : 8 and 9 : 12 are **equivalent ratios**.

- Find **equivalent ratios** by multiplying or dividing both numbers in a ratio by the same number:

> $3 : 4 = 3 \times 2 : 4 \times 2 = \mathbf{6 : 8}$
> $3 : 4 = 3 \times 3 : 4 \times 3 = \mathbf{9 : 2}$

- Share an amount in a ratio.

Example: Pam plants daffodils to crocuses in the ratio 5 : 9.
She has 42 bulbs in total. How many of each bulb does she plant?

> For every 5 daffodils, there are 9 crocuses. 14 bulbs in total.
> Or, for every 10 daffodils, 18 crocuses. 28 bulbs in total.
> Or, for every 15 daffodils, 27 crocuses. 42 bulbs in total

Test yourself

1 Fill in the gaps to make equivalent ratios:

a) 4 : 3 = ___ : 6 c) 7 : 1 = ___ : 5 e) 2 : 3 = ___ : 18
b) 2 : 5 = 6 : ___ d) 8 : 9 = 32 : ___ f) 5 : 8 = 30 : ___

2 Julie makes a fruit drink with oranges to lemons, 2 : 1.
Julie buys 6 oranges. How many lemons does she buy?

3 Green paint is mixed in the ratio blue to yellow, 1 : 4. Carmela wants to make 20 litres of green paint.
a) How many litres of blue paint does Carmela need?
b) How many litres of yellow paint does Carmela need?
c) How much blue and yellow paint is needed for 40 litres of paint?

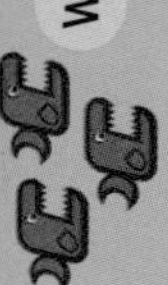

Check the facts

Algebra uses letters that stand for unknown numbers.

A letter on its own or multiplied by a number or another letter is called a **term**.

Examples: p, $3a$ and xy are all terms.

Remember: a number and a letter or a letter and a letter multiplied together do not have a multiplication sign. So, $3a$ is 3 multiplied by a and xy is x multiplied by y.

Terms joined by + − × or ÷ make algebraic expressions.

Examples: $a + b$, $4x - y$, $\frac{5p}{r}$ are all algebraic expressions.

$a + b$ means a number, a, add another number, b.

$4x - y$ means 4 lots of a number, x, subtract a number, y.

$\frac{5p}{r}$ means 5 lots of a number, p, divide by a number, r.

Examples:

The cost of an ice-cream is m and the cost of a topping is n.

- Order a single cornet and $m = 0.8$ (£0.80).
- Choose a nut topping and $n = 0.3$ (£0.30).
- Peter orders a single cornet with a nut topping. So, $m + n = 0.8 + 0.3 = 1.1$. That is £1.10. Peter's ice-cream costs £1.10.
- Simon is x years old. Simon's brother is 4 years younger. So, Simon's brother is $x - 4$ years old.
- Simon's father is three times as old as Simon. So, he is $3x$ years old.

Test yourself

1 Write down the algebraic expression that says:

a) three lots of a number s

b) a number q subtract a number t

c) seven lots of a number y add a number z.

2 Millie has n cards for Valentine's Day.

a) Charlie has twice as many cards as Millie.

b) Jake has one more card than Millie.

c) Pippa has two less cards than Millie.

Write the algebraic expressions that say how many cards Charlie, Jake and Pippa received.

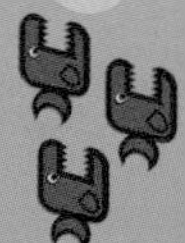

Check the facts

Terms made up of the same letter are called like terms.

Simplify algebraic expressions by adding or subtracting **like terms**.

Examples: $p + 7p = 8p$ $6v - v = 5v$ $11m + 2m = 13m$

Notice that where a letter is on its own in algebra, you do not write 1 in front of it. So, p ✓ $1p$ ✗ $-v$ ✓ $-1v$ ✗

Sometimes, **like terms** appear among other terms. Group **like terms** together, then add or subtract them.

Examples: $4y + 3x + y = 4y + y + 3x = 5y + 3x$

$6a + 2b + 2a - b = 6a + 2a + 2b - b = 8a + b$

Notice that only **like terms** can be added or subtracted.

The algebraic expression $2r + 5s - 4q + 7t$ cannot be simplified, because $2r$, $5s$, $-4q$, $7t$ are unlike terms.

Sometimes an algebraic expression has brackets. Brackets mean multiply. Simplify an algebraic expression with brackets by multiplying the number next to a bracket by all the terms inside the bracket.

Examples:

$2(3t - 4)$ $2 \times 3t = 6t$ and $2 \times -4 = -8$

so, $2(3t - 4) = 6t - 8$

$3(5f + 2g)$ $3 \times 5f = 15f$ and $3 \times 2g = 6g$

so, $3(5f + 2g) = 15f + 6g$

Test yourself

1 Simplify the following expressions:

a) $4j + 3j$ c) $7e - 4e + 10e$ e) $9x + 6y - 4x - y$

b) $6k - k - 4i$ d) $5a - 3 + 2b + 12a$ f) $5(2c + 4)$

2 A flat is sold for £x.
The house next door is sold for four times as much as the flat.
The bungalow next door is sold for three times as much as the flat.
The sports car opposite is sold for half the price of the flat.
How much were the three properties and car sold for in total, in terms of x?

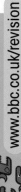

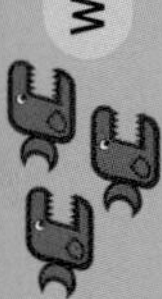

Check the facts

A formula is a rule that can be applied to a number to give a new number.

Sometimes **formulae** are shown as number machines. A number goes into the machine, a rule acts on it and out comes a new number.

Example: in 12 → − 8 → out 4 in 20 → ÷ 4 → out 5

Sometimes different numbers are put into the same number machine.

Example: in 7 → − 3 → out 4 in 13 → − 3 → out 10

A number goes in, 3 is subtracted from the number and a new number comes out. The number that goes in varies.

It is a variable. Let's call the variable x: x → − 3 → $x - 3$

Sometimes a number machine will use more than one rule.

Example:

in 15 → ÷ 3 → + 4 → out 9 in p → × 2 → − 3 → out $2p-3$

Test yourself

Fill in the gaps in these number machines:

1 11 → + 5 → ____

2 28 → ÷ 7 → ____

3 z → − 4 → ____

4 ____ → + 9 → $a + 9$

5 p → ____ → $6p$

6 10 → × 3 → − 8 → ____

7 16 → − 2 → ÷ 7 → ____

8 b → ÷ 3 → + 4 → ____

9 x → − 1 → ____ → $\frac{x-1}{6}$

10 d → ____ → + 9 → $5d + 9$

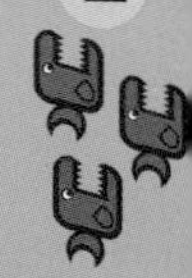

Substitution

Check the facts

As different numbers are substituted into a formula the value of the formula changes.

Examples:

- Cooking time for turkey = 40 × weight (kg) + 20 = $40w + 20$

If w = 2	If w = 8
then cooking time = $40w + 20$	then cooking time = $40w + 20$
= 40 × 2 + 20	= 40 × 8 + 20
= 100 minutes	= 340 minutes

- Area of a triangle = $\frac{1}{2}$ × base × height = $\frac{1}{2}bh$

If b = 5 cm and h = 4 cm	If b = 3 cm and h = 8 cm
then area = $\frac{1}{2}bh$	then area = $\frac{1}{2}bh$
= $\frac{1}{2}$ × 5 × 4	= $\frac{1}{2}$ × 3 × 8
= 10 cm^2	= 12 cm^2

- Find the value of 3 (d + 6) when d = 4 and when d = 6.

Remember: brackets mean multiply.

If $d = 4$
then 3 (d + 6) =
3 (4 + 6) =
3 × 10 = 30

Test yourself

1 This formula is used to find the cost of servicing a car:
cost = £45 + 10 × number of hours
$c = 45 + 10n$
Find c when (a) $n = 1$ (b) $n = 3$ (c) $n = \frac{1}{2}$

2 Find the value of $5y + 7$ when (a) $y = 6$ (b) $y = 9$

3 Find the value of $16 - 3j$ when (a) $j = 2$ (b) $j = 5$

4 Find the value of $4(2k + 1)$ when (a) $k = 3$ (b) $k = 4$

5 Find the value of $3(5b - 4)$ when (a) $b = 3$ (b) $b = 2$

Check the facts

An **equation** has an equals sign and an unknown number written as a letter. The equals sign lets you solve the equation to find the unknown number.

If you are confident with a method of solving equations and it works, use it! If not, then here is one method using inverse operations:

> **Inverse** means opposite:
> - the inverse of **add** is **subtract**, so inverse of **+ 6** is **– 6**
> - the inverse of **subtract** is **add**, so inverse of **– 3** is **+ 3**
> - the inverse of **multiply** is **divide**, so inverse of × 4 is ÷ 4
> - the inverse of **divide** is **multiply**, so inverse of ÷ 9 is × 9

Examples:

Take 2, use the rule **+ 7** to get 9: 2 ⟶ + 7 ⟶ 9

Take 9, apply inverse rule **– 7** to get 2: 9 ⟶ – 7 ⟶ 2

Take 3, use the rule **× 2 – 5** to get 1: 3 ⟶ × 2 – 5 ⟶ 1

Take 1, apply inverse rule **+ 5 ÷ 2** to get 3: 1 ⟶ + 5 ÷ 2 ⟶ 3

In an equation, apply the inverse rule to find the unknown number.

Examples:

Find the value of y if $y - 6 = 8$ y ⟶ – 6 ⟶ 8

Take 8, apply inverse rule + **6** to get y: 8 ⟶ + 6 ⟶ y

$8 + 6 = y$, so, $y = 14$

(**Check**: $y - 6 = 8$. If $y = 14$, then $14 - 6 = 8$✓)

Test yourself

1 What is the inverse of these rules:

a) + 4 b) ÷ 11 c) × 5 d) – 1 × 6 e) ÷ 3 – 9 f) + 6 ÷ 4?

2 Solve these equations to find the unknown numbers.

a) $r + 4 = 9$ d) $d + 6 = 15$ g) $3z - 5 = 16$
b) $m - 2 = 3$ e) $2c + 1 = 5$ h) $2b + 6 = 16$
c) $p - 7 = 13$ f) $3a - 8 = 10$ i) $8n - 3 = 45$

Equations

BBC KS3 Check and Test: Maths

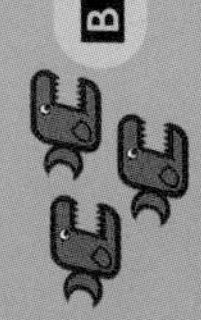

More equations

Check the facts

There may be some work to do before solving an equation.

There may be terms to collect. If there are **like terms**, simplify by collecting them together. Then solve the equation.

Example: Solve $5x - 7 - x = 13$

Simplify: $5x - 7 - x = 5x - x - 7 = 13$

That is $4x - 7 = 13$ $\quad$ $x \rightarrow \times 4 - 7 \rightarrow 13$

Apply the **inverse rule** $+ 7 \div 4$ $\quad$ $13 \rightarrow + 7 \div 4 \rightarrow x$

$13 + 7 \div 4 = x$, so $x = 5$

(Check: $5x - 7 - x = 5 \times 5 - 7 - 5 = 25 - 7 - 5 = 13$)

There may be brackets. If there are brackets, simplify by multiplying the number next to the bracket by all the terms inside the bracket. Then solve the equation.

Example: Solve $4(2b + 1) = 28$

Simplify: $4(2b + 1) = 4 \times 2b + 4 \times 1 = 28$

That is $8b + 4 = 28$ $\quad$ $b \rightarrow \times 8 + 4 \rightarrow 28$

Apply the **inverse rule** $- 4 \div 8$: $\quad$ $28 \rightarrow - 4 \div 8 \rightarrow b$

$28 - 4 \div 8 = b$, so $b = 3$

(Check: $4(2b + 1) = 28$. If $b = 3$, then $4(6 + 1) = 28$✓)

Test yourself

Solve these equations to find the unknown numbers.

1. $3p + 8 - 2p = 12$
2. $8t - 9 + 2t = 31$
3. $2(5q - 3) = 14$
4. $4(2s + 5) = 100$
5. $3(4 + 2x) = 60$
6. $10 + 3y + 4y = 52$
7. $7n - 2n - 22 = 13$
8. $3(2f + 6) = 30$
9. $4 + 4j - 5 + 7j = 21$
10. $6 + 8r - 2 - 3r = 19$

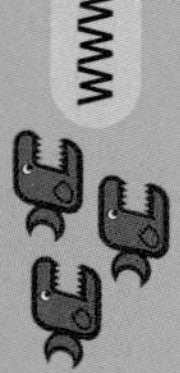

Check the facts

Equations can be used to solve word problems.

Examples:

- Emma is y years old. Emma's brother, James, is four years younger. Add together Emma's age and James's age and you get their mother's age, 42. How old are Emma and James?

> Emma is y years old.
> James is four years younger, that's $y - 4$ years old.
> Add Emma's age and James's age to get 42.
> So, the equation is $y + y - 4 = 42$.
> Simplify: $y + y - 4 = 2y - 4 = 42$
> Now solve: $y \longrightarrow \times 2 - 4 \longrightarrow 42$
> Apply the **inverse rule** $+ 4 \div 2$: $42 \longrightarrow + 4 \div 2 \longrightarrow y$
> $42 + 4 \div 2 = 23$, **so $y = 23$**
> Emma's age is 23 and **James's age is 23 – 4 = 19.**

- Mr Sol buys a newspaper for n pence each weekday. On Fridays, Mrs Sol has *YES!* magazine. It costs £2. At the end of the week, the Sols pay the newsagent £3.25. How much is Mr Sol's newspaper?

> Mr Sol has a newspaper each weekday, five days a week.
> It costs n pence each day, that's $5n$ per week.
> Add on Mrs Sol's magazine: $5n + 2$.
> Mr and Mrs Sol pay the newsagent £3.25.
> So, the equation is $5n + 2 = 3.25$.
> Now solve: $n \longrightarrow \times 5 + 2 \longrightarrow 3.25$
> Apply the **inverse rule** $- 2 \div 5$: $3.25 \longrightarrow - 2 \div 5 \longrightarrow n$
> $3.25 - 2 \div 5 = n$, **so n = £0.25**
> Mr Sol's newspaper is £0.25 or **25 pence.**

Test yourself

1 Gary is z years old. His sister is twice as old. The sum of their ages is 27. How old is Gary?

2 Sharminee thinks of a number, n. She multiplies the number by 4 then adds 3 to it. Her answer is 35. What number did Sharminee start with?

3 Ken has two packets of biscuits. Each packet contains the same number of biscuits. Ken eats three biscuits and has 57 left. How many biscuits were in each packet?

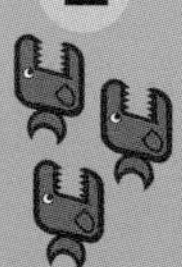

What is an inequality?

Check the facts

An **inequality** shows that a variable may be **less than** or **greater than** a number. Here are the four kinds of inequality signs:

$<$ 'less than'	$>$ 'greater than'
$\leqslant$ 'less than or equal to'	$\geqslant$ 'greater than or equal to'

Examples: $p < 2$ — p is less than 2, or 2 is greater than p

$k > 1$ — k is greater than 1, or 1 is less than k

- More than one inequality sign may appear in an expression.

Example: $3 < x < 7$ — x is greater than 3 and less than 7

Assuming x is a whole number, then x must be 4, 5 or 6.

- Apply the same rule (add, subtract, multiply or divide by a positive number) to each side of any inequality and the inequality will still be true.

Example: $3 < 7$ — 3 is less than 7. True!

Apply rule + 2 to both sides: $3 + 2 < 7 + 2$, so $5 < 9$. True!

Apply rule × 3 to both sides: $3 \times 3 < 7 \times 3$, so $9 < 21$. True!

- Here is one method of solving inequalities using inverse rules applied to both sides:

Example: $y - 4 < 9$ — y subtract 4 is less than 9

The rule is – 4, so apply inverse rule + 4 to both sides:

$y - 4 + 4 < 9 + 4$, so $y < 13$, y is a number less than 13.

Test yourself

1 Write these inequalities using the correct sign:

a) a is greater than or equal to 6

b) b is less than 9

c) c is less than or equal to 10

d) 5 is greater than d

2 List whole number values of p in each inequality:

a) $2 \leqslant p \leqslant 5$ b) $0 < p < 3$ c) $7 > p \geqslant 4$

d) $-1 \leqslant p > 3$ e) $4 > p > -2$ f) $-3 \leqslant p \leqslant 0$

3 Solve these inequalities:

a) $3r \leqslant 12$ b) $2c > 16$ c) $\frac{j}{2} < 10$

Check the facts

A **number pattern** is a series or chain of numbers that follow a rule. The **rule** may be add, subtract, multiply or divide the same number each time.

> **Examples:** 30, 25, 20, 15 . . . follows the rule 'subtract 5'.
> The next number in the pattern is 15 – 5 = 10.
>
> 3, 6, 12, 24 . . . follows the rule 'multiply by 2'.
> The next number in the pattern is 24 × 2 = 48.

A number pattern may be shown using diagrams.

Example: See the pattern grow.

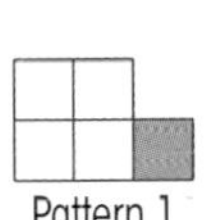

Pattern 1

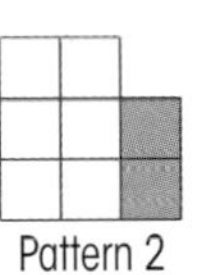

Pattern 2

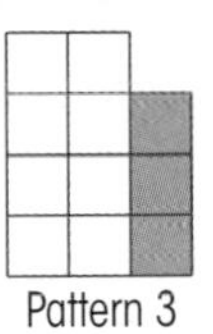

Pattern 3

Pattern 1 has 1 orange tile and 4 white tiles.
Pattern 2 has 2 orange tiles and 6 white tiles.
Pattern 3 has 3 orange tiles and 8 white tiles.
The number pattern for grey tiles is 1, 2, 3 . . .
It follows the rule **add 1**. The next number is 3 + 1 = 4.
The number pattern for white tiles is 4, 6, 8 . . .
It follows the rule **add 2**. The next number is 8 + 2 = 10.

Test yourself

1 Find the rule and the next number in each of these number patterns:

a) 5, 8, 11, 14 . . .
b) 5, 10, 20, 40 . . .
c) 32, 16, 8, 4 . . .
d) 7, 12, 19, 24 . . .
e) 250, 50, 10, 5 . . .
f) 22, 18, 14, 10 . . .

2 Anne has white triangular tiles. Katie has grey triangular tiles. They make this series of patterns:

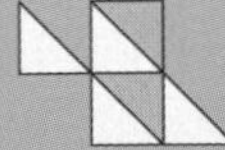

Pattern 1

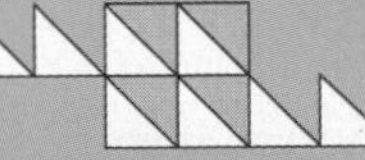

Pattern 2

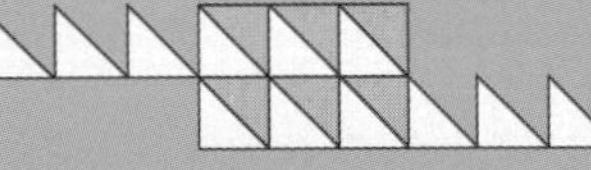

Pattern 3

a) How many grey tiles does Katie add each time?
b) How many white tiles does Anne add each time?

Anne and Katie make Pattern 4.

c) How many white tiles does Anne need?
d) How many grey tiles does Katie need?

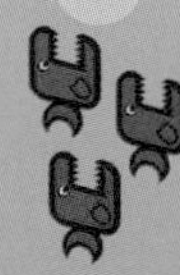

Check the facts

Rather than finding the next number in a number pattern, you may want to find the 19th or 54th number. Writing out 19 or 54 numbers in a pattern takes a long time, so it is useful to find a general rule, the ***n*th term**.

Example: 2, 4, 6 . . . 2 4 6 . . . (+2 +2) the rule is 'add 2'

this is the two times table

the 1st term is $2 = \mathbf{2} \times \mathbf{1}$

the **2nd term** is $4 = 2 + 2 = \mathbf{2} \times \mathbf{2}$

the **3rd term** is $6 = 2 + 2 + 2 = \mathbf{2} \times \mathbf{3}$

Notice that each time, 2 is multiplied by its **term number**.

So, the nth term is: $2 \times n$, or $2n$.

Now any term can be found using this general rule, $2n$.

For the 19th term, $n = 19$: $2n = 2 \times 19 = 38$

> All times tables can be written in terms of n.
>
> For the **three times table** ('add 3'), the general rule is $3n$.
>
> For the **four times table** ('add 4'), the general rule is $4n$.

Look at this number pattern: 5 9 13 17.

The rule is 'add 4': +4 +4 +4

But it is not the four times table: 4 8 12 16 $4n$

Each term in 5, 9, 13, 17 . . . is the four times table add 1.

So, the nth term of 5, 9, 13, 17 . . . . is $4n + 1$.

For the 10th term, $n = 10$: $4n + 1 = 4 \times 10 + 1 = 41$

Test yourself

1 Find the general rule (nth term) for these number patterns:

a) 6, 12, 18, 24 . . .
b) 9, 18, 27, 36 . . .
c) 7, 14, 21, 28 . . .
d) 3, 5, 7, 9 . . .
e) 1, 5, 9, 13 . . .
f) 4, 10, 16, 22 . . .
g) 2, 5, 8, 11 . . .
h) 9, 16, 23, 30 . . .

2 Find the 5th and 10th terms for the number patterns a to h.

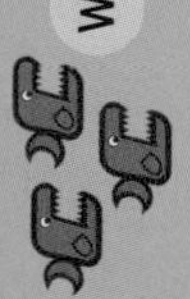

Check the facts

The horizontal axis is the x-axis.
The vertical axis is the y-axis.

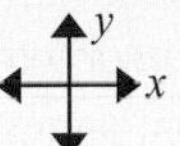

Remember: the horizontal axis is across, and x is a cross.

Coordinates mark a point on a grid.
Read or plot coordinates by starting at (0, 0), the **origin**.

move across **right** or across **left** first:
right → for positive x-numbers, left ← for negative x-numbers.

then move **up** or **down**:
up ↑ for positive y-numbers, down ↓ for negative y-numbers.

Write coordinates like this: (x-coordinate, y-coordinate).

Look at this grid:

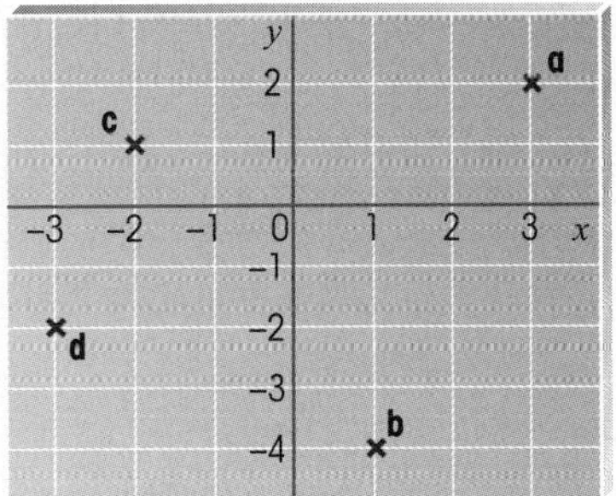

Coordinate a: start at (0,0) move across right → 3 then move up ↑ 2 the coordinates are (3, 2)	Coordinate b: start at (0,0) move across right 1 then move down 4 the coordinates are (1, –4)
Coordinate c: start at (0,0) move across left 2 then move up 1 the coordinates are (–2, 1)	Coordinate d: start at (0,0) move across left 3 then move down 2 the coordinates are (–3, –2)

Test yourself

1 Look at the triangle drawn on this grid:
Write the coordinates of each vertex (corner) of the triangle, points A, B, C.

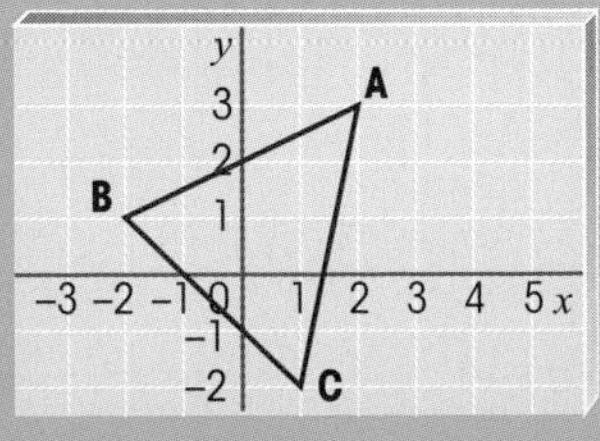

Line graphs

BBC KS3 Check and Test: Maths

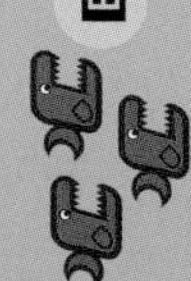

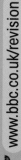

Mappings

Check the facts

A **mapping** is a rule that works on a number to give a new number. Mappings may be represented as diagrams.

Examples:

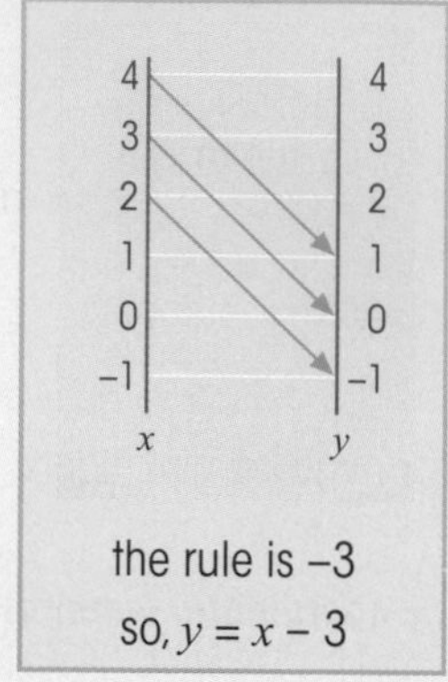

the rule is −3
so, $y = x - 3$

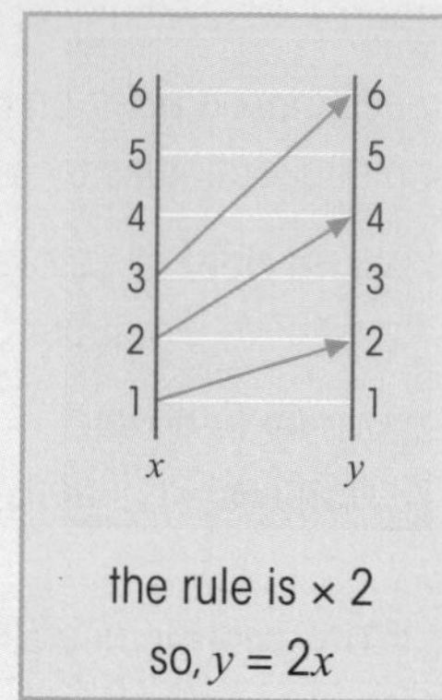

the rule is × 2
so, $y = 2x$

Mappings give coordinates that can be plotted on a grid.

Examples:

$y = x - 3$ gives coordinates (2, − 1), (3, 0) and (4, 1).
$y = 2x$ gives coordinates (1, 2), (2, 4) and (3, 6).

These coordinates give straight-line graphs:

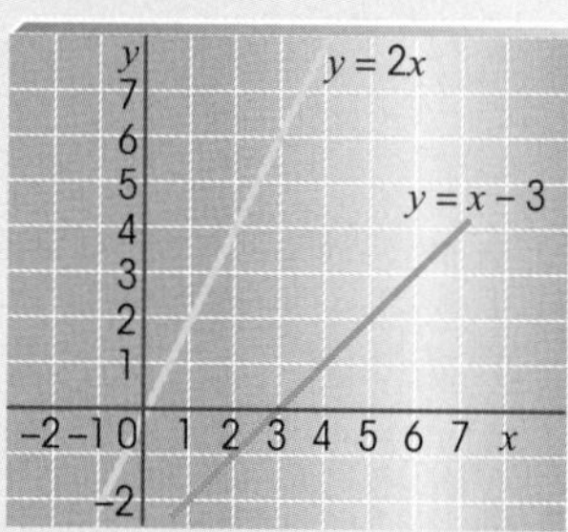

Test yourself

1 Copy and complete these mapping diagrams for $x = 0$, $x = 1$ and $x = 2$:

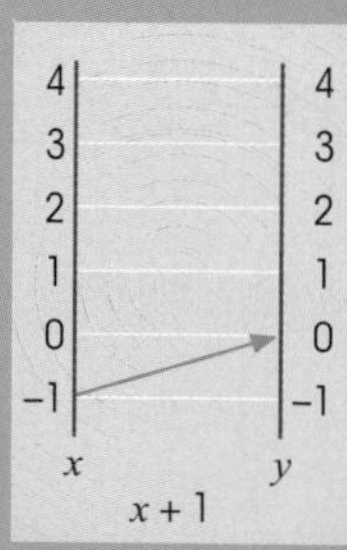

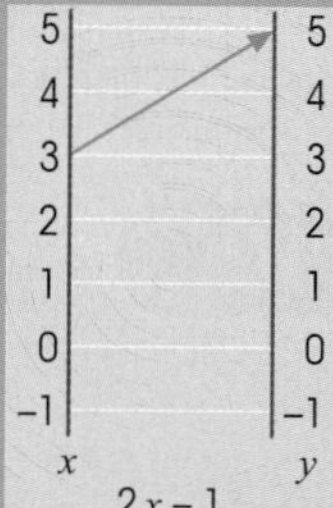

2 Write three pairs of coordinates for each of the equations:
a) $y = x + 1$ b) $y = x - 2$

Check the facts

The minimum number of points needed to draw a straight-line graph is two:

Find three points and the third point acts as a check:

So, find three points to draw the straight-line graph of an equation. Choose three values of x and substitute these x-values into the equation to find corresponding y coordinates. (See section 41: 'Substitution' as a reminder.)

Example:

Draw the graph of $y = x + 1$ for values x from 0 to 4.

Choose three values of x: $x = 0, x = 1, x = 2$

Substitute in the equation $y = x + 1$:

x	0	1	2
y	1	2	3

when $x = 0$,
$y = 0 + 1 = 1$

when $x = 1$,
$y = 1 + 1 = 2$

when $x = 2$,
$y = 2 + 1 = 3$

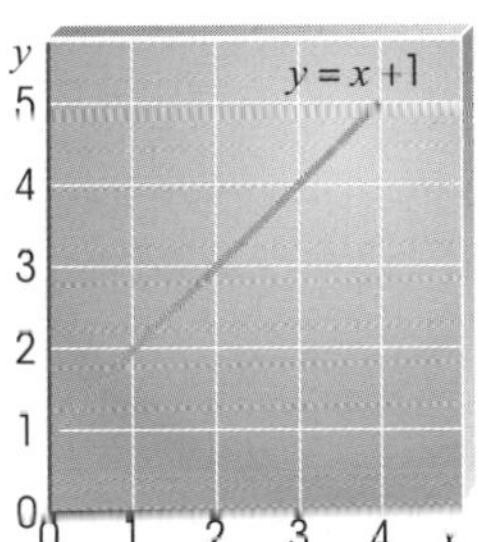

Test yourself

1 Complete these tables to find coordinates of equations:

a) $y = x - 2$

x	**0**	**2**	**4**
y	**−2**		

b) $y = x + 2$

x	**−1**	**0**	**2**
y	**1**		

c) $y = \frac{1}{2}x - 1$

x	**−2**	**0**	**2**
y	**−2**		

2 a) Draw graph $y = x - 2$ for values of x from 0 to 4.
b) Draw graph $y = x + 2$ for values of x from −2 to 2.
c) Draw graph $y = 1–2\ x - 1$ for values of x from −2 to 3.

3 Draw these graphs for values of x from −2 to 2:
a) $y = x - 1$
b) $y = 2x - 2$

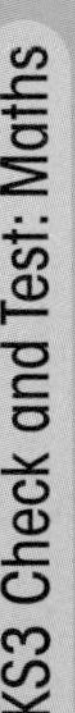

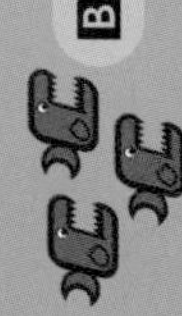

Check the facts

Gradient measures the **steepness** of a line.

gradient = distance up or down ÷ distance along

Measure distance along to the right ⟶, then

if you go up ↑, the gradient is **positive**

if you go down ↓, the gradient is **negative**.

Examples:

Line A

A: count 2 along and 1 up, so gradient = $\frac{1}{2}$

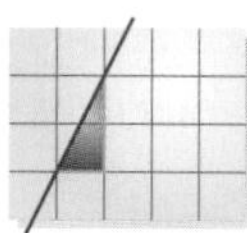

Line B

B: count 1 along and 2 up, so gradient = $\frac{2}{1} = 2$

Notice that it does not matter where you count to, you always calculate the same gradient for the same line.

Examples:

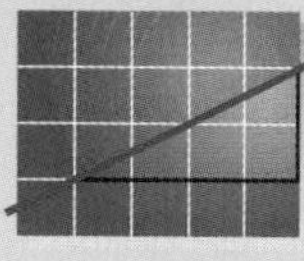

Line A

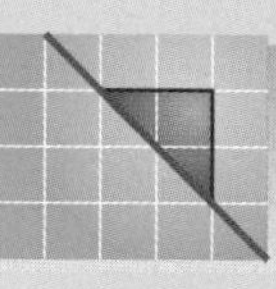

Line B

A: count 4 along and 2 up
gradient = $\frac{2}{4} = \frac{1}{2}$ (cancelled down)

B: count 2 along and 2 down
gradient = $-\frac{2}{2} = -1$

Sometimes gradients are written as **percentages** The gradient is written as a fraction of 100.

Example: 10% = $\frac{10}{100} = \frac{1}{10}$ (cancelled down)
(For 10 units travelled along, you go one unit up. That is 10 cm along and 1 cm up, or 10 m along and 1 m up, and so on.)

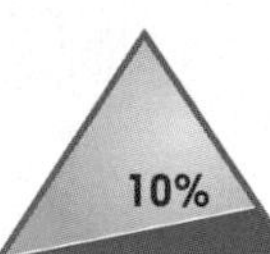

Test yourself

1 Find the gradients of these lines:

a) 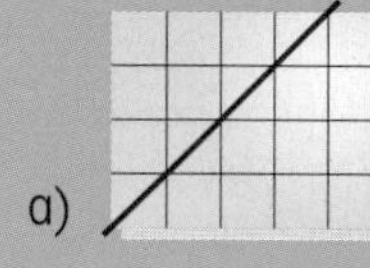 b) 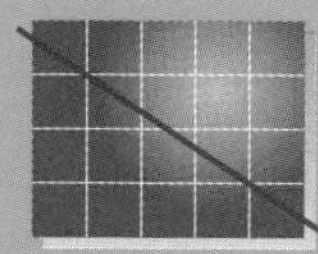 c)

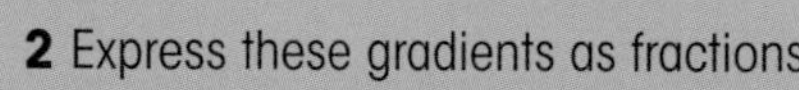

2 Express these gradients as fractions:

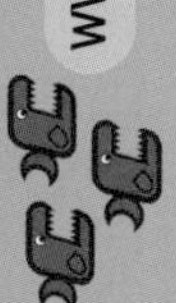

a) 

b) 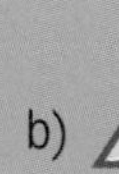 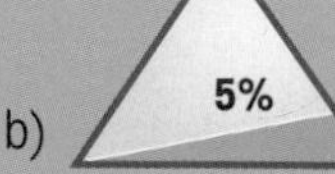

c) 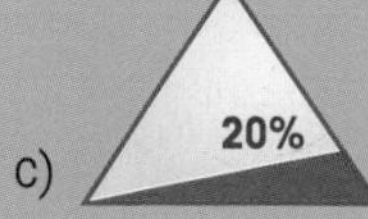

Check the facts

Look at this equation: $y = 3x + 1$

It is written as:

y = a number multiplied by x + another number

Any equation written like this can be shown as a straight-line graph:

- the number multiplied by x is the **gradient**
- the other number is the **intercept** (intercept is where the graph crosses the y-axis).

Examples:

$y = 3x + 1$ has gradient 3 and intercept +1 (crosses the y-axis at $y = 1$).
So, mark a point at $y = 1$.
Gradient is 3, so move 1 across and up 3 then 1 across and up 3.

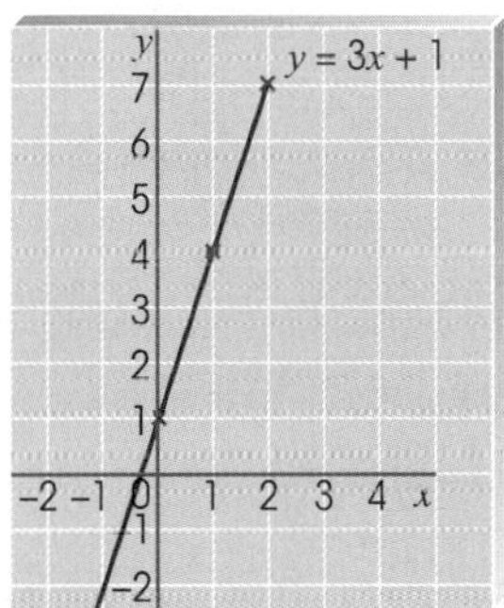

This is the straight-line graph of the equation $y = 3x + 1$.

Test yourself

1 Find the gradient and intercept for the straight-line graphs of the following equations:

a) $y = 4x + 1$
b) $y = 2x - 3$
c) $y = 3x + 2$
d) $y = \frac{1}{2}x - 2$
e) $y = -x + 4$
f) $y = -3x + 2$

2 Copy this grid onto a large piece of graph paper and draw the straight-line graphs of equations 1a) to 1f).

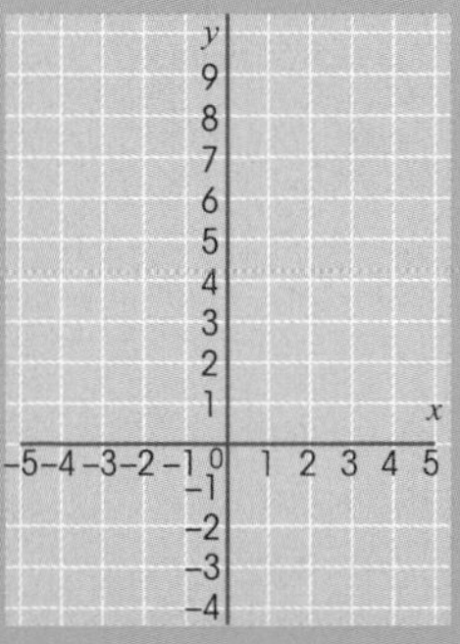

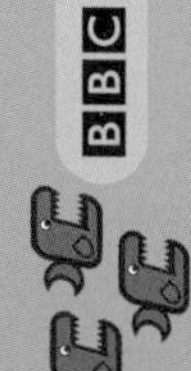

53

Finding the equation of a straight-line graph

Check the facts

Remember! Straight-line graphs of equations are written as:

y = gradient multiplied by x + or – intercept

gradient: distance up or down ÷ distance along

intercept: where the graph crosses the y-axis

Look at this graph:

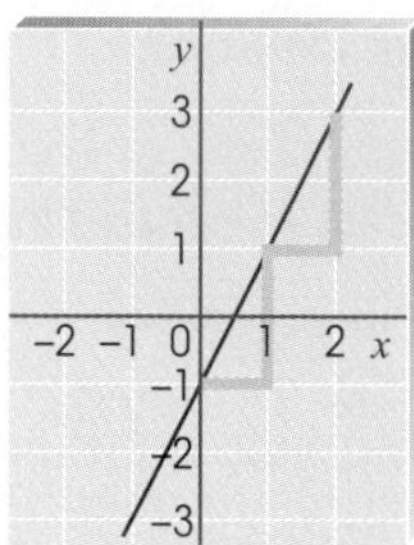

Count one along and two up, so gradient = $\frac{2}{1}$ = 2.

The graph crosses the y-axis at $y = -1$, intercept = –1.

So, the equation of the graph is $y = 2x - 1$.

Test yourself

1 Find the gradient and intercept of each of the following straight-line graphs:

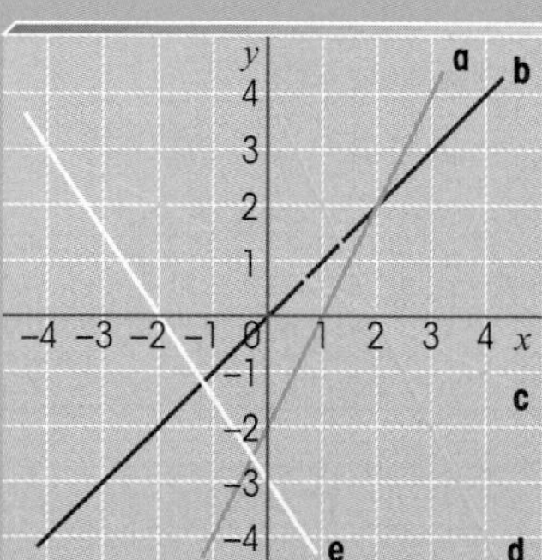

2 Write the equation of each of the graphs 1(a) to 1(e).

Check the facts

Lines are **parallel** if they are always the same distance apart. That means the lines never meet.

These three lines are parallel:

These two lines are parallel:

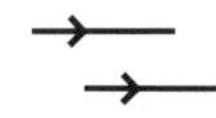

The small arrows on the lines show they are parallel.

- Look at these straight-line graphs:

  The lines $y = x + 2$
  $y = x + 1$
  $y = x - 2$
  are **parallel**.

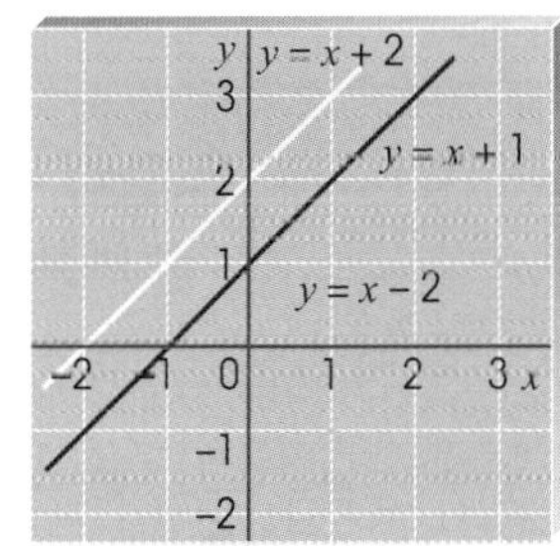

- Notice that parallel-line graphs have the same gradient. $y = x + 2$, $y = x + 1$ and $y = x - 2$ have gradient 1.
- But parallel-line graphs cross the y-axis at different points.

> Say you wanted to draw the straight-line graph $y = -2x - 1$.
>
> The straight-line graph $y = -2x - 1$ is parallel to the straight-line graphs $y = -2x + 3$, $y = -2x + 1$ and $y = -2x$.
>
> The straight-line graph $y = -2x - 1$ crosses the y-axis at -1.

Test yourself

1 Look at the straight-line graphs opposite. Fill in the gaps to show which line is which equation.

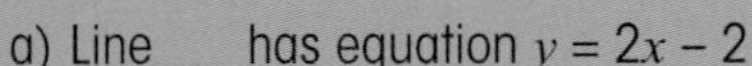

a) Line___ has equation $y = 2x - 2$.

b) Line___ has equation $y = x$.

c) Line___ has equation $y = 2x + 2$.

d) Line___ has equation $y = x + 2$.

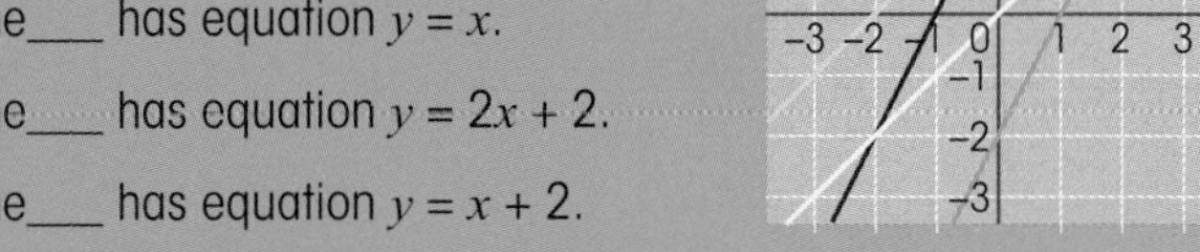

2 Copy the grid and graphs above and then draw these lines:

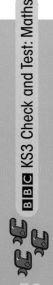

a) $y = x - 1$ b) $y = x + 3$ c) $y = x - 3$

Line graphs

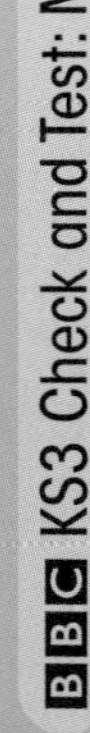

Check the facts

An angle measures a turn, or a rotation, in degrees (°).

Angles measuring exactly 90° are **right angled**.

Example:

Notice the small square shows the right angle.

Angles measuring 0° to 90° are **acute**.

Example:

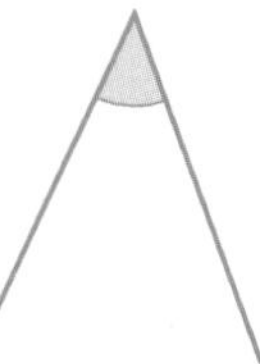

Angles measuring 90° to 180° are **obtuse**.

Example:

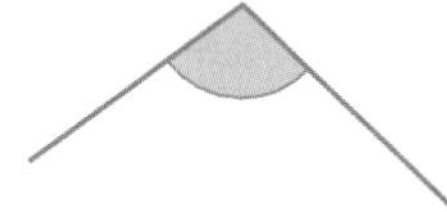

Angles measuring 180° to 360° are **reflex**.

Example:

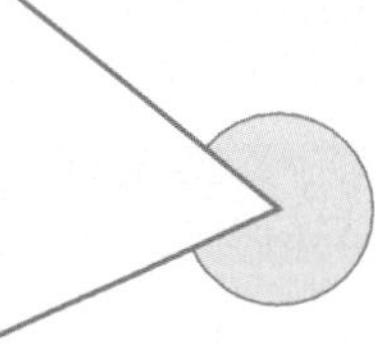

Test yourself

1 Label the following angles: right angled, acute, obtuse or reflex.

a) 46° b) 270° c) 109° d) 189° e) f)

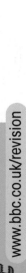

2 Match each angle to its correct angle size:

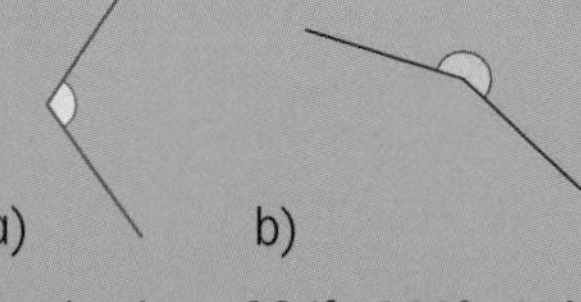

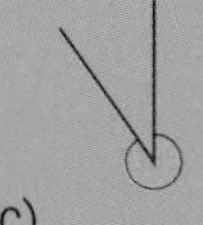

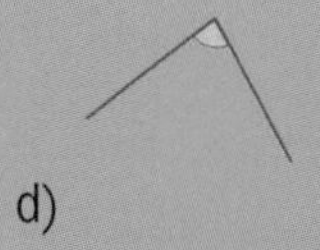

a) b) c) d)

angle sizes: 206°, 112°, 80°, 325°

Check the facts

Measure angles accurately using a **protractor**.

- Place the protractor over the angle, with its base line on one of the arms of the angle.
- The point of the angle must be exactly under the centre of the protractor.
- Follow the scale from 0° round to where the other arm of the angle meets the scale. Read the number of degrees.

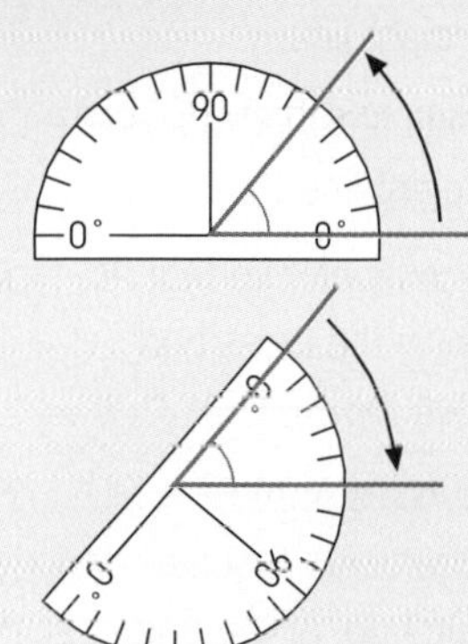

If an angle is reflex, it may be easier to use a circular protractor.

Examples: Measure this angle. (**Notice**: the angle is obtuse, so expect a measurement between 90° and 180°.)

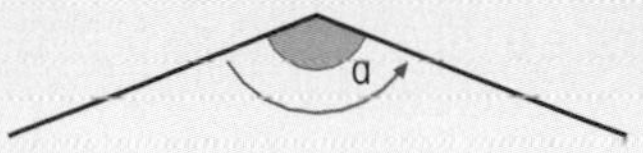

Measure from 0° in the direction of the arrow.

The angle is 139°.

Test yourself

Measure these angles (you must be accurate to within 1°).

1

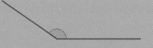

2

3

4

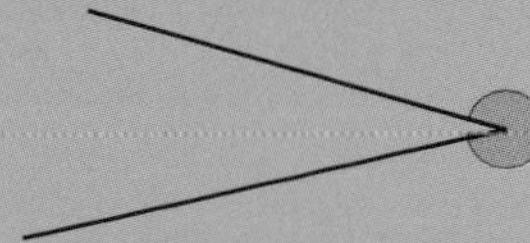

Drawing angles accurately

Check the facts

Draw angles accurately using a ruler and a protractor.

- Draw a straight line.
- Mark a small cross (x) anywhere on the straight line.
- Place the protractor so that its centre is over the cross and 90° is above the cross.
- Follow the scale from 0° round to the angle required and mark a small dot at the angle.
- Move the protractor away, join the cross and the dot and mark the angle.

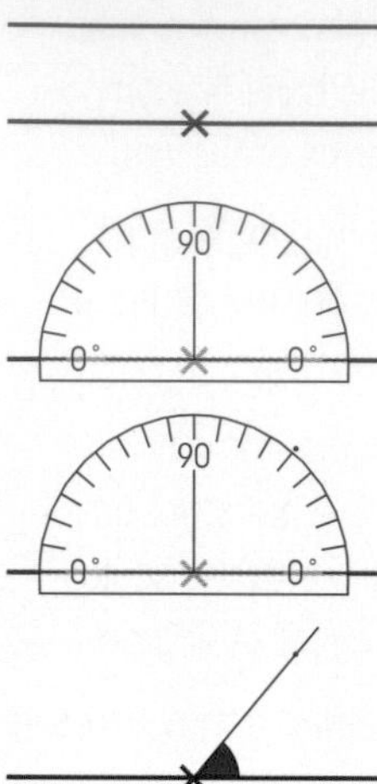

If an angle is reflex, it may be easier to use a circular protractor.

Examples: Draw these angles: angle **a**: 114° angle **b**: 290°

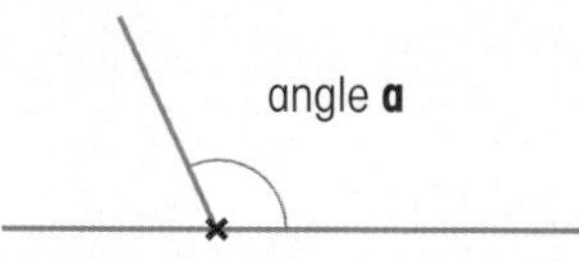

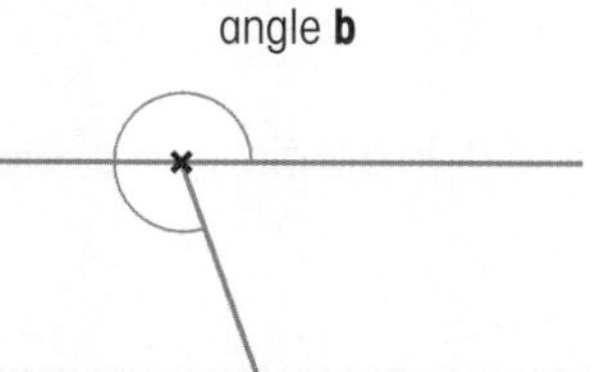

Follow the scale from 0° round to 114°.

Follow the scale from 0° round to 290°.

> As a check, make sure that your angle looks correct.
> Angle **a** looks like an obtuse angle between 90° and 180°. ✔
> Angle **b** looks like a reflex angle between 180° and 360°. ✔

Test yourself

Draw these angles (you must be accurate to within 1°).
(You could draw the angles on tracing paper to make it easy to check them against the answers at the back of the book.)

1 27° **2** 90° **3** 189° **4** 260° **5** 35° **6** 305° **7** 64° **8** 100°

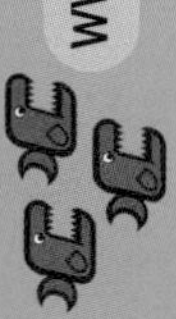

Check the facts

Angles on a straight line add up to 180°.

Example:

50° 130°

50° + 130° = 180°

Calculate the missing angle on a straight line by subtracting the known angle or angles from 180°.

Example:

72° 60° **q**

q = 180° – 72° – 60° = 48°

Angles around a point add up to 360°.

Example:

90° 210° 60°

90° + 210° + 60° = 360°

Calculate the missing angle around a point by subtracting the known angle or angles from 360°.

Example:

125° 128° **s**

s = 360° – 125° – 128° = 107°

Test yourself

You may use your calculator to help you.

1 Calculate the missing angles in the following diagrams:

2 Calculate the value of x by forming an equation and then solving it. **Remember!** All angles around a point add up to 360°.

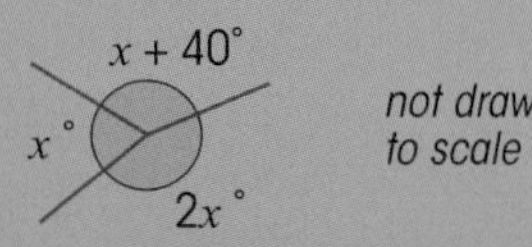

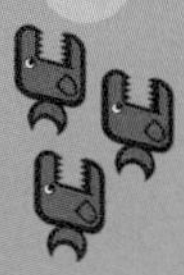

Angles made by intersecting straight lines

Check the facts

When two straight lines **intersect** (cut each other), the **opposite** angles are equal.

Example:

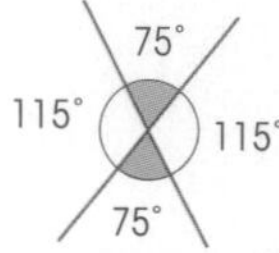

A **transversal** is a straight line that intersects (cuts) parallel lines.

Remember: lines are parallel if they are always the same perpendicular distance apart. **Parallel lines never meet**.

The F-shape of a transversal makes equal **corresponding** angles.

Example:

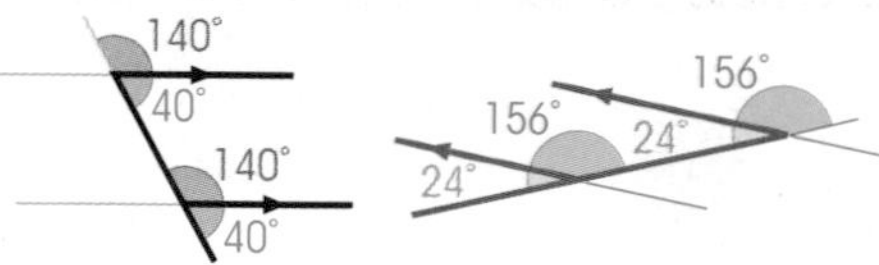

The Z-shape of a transversal makes equal **alternate** angles.

Example:

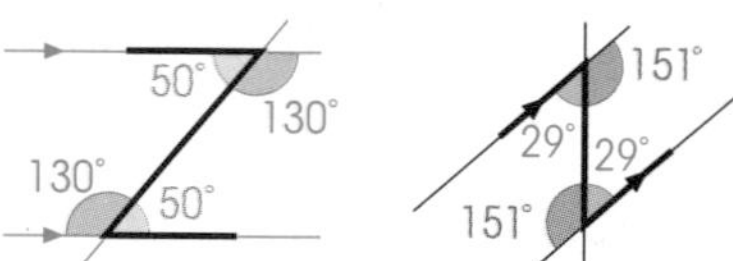

Interior angles of a transversal add up to 180°.

Example:

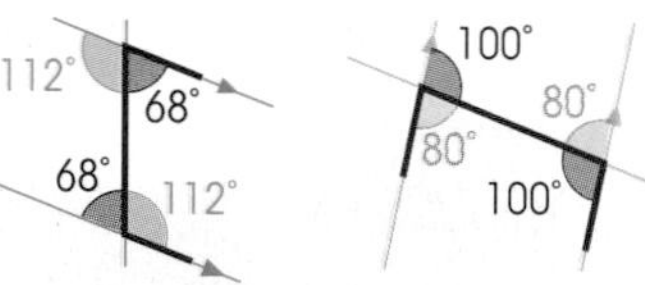

Test yourself

Find the value of the missing angle in each of these diagrams, stating the reason (opposite, corresponding, alternate or interior angles).

1

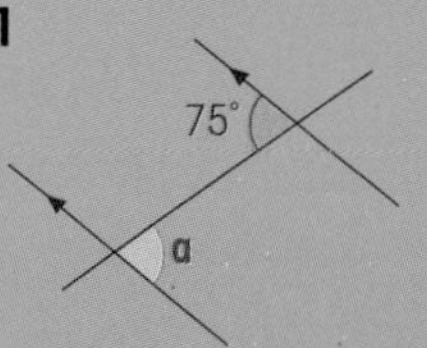

2

3

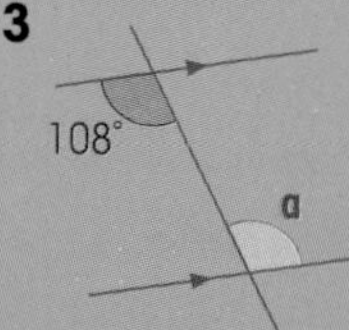

4

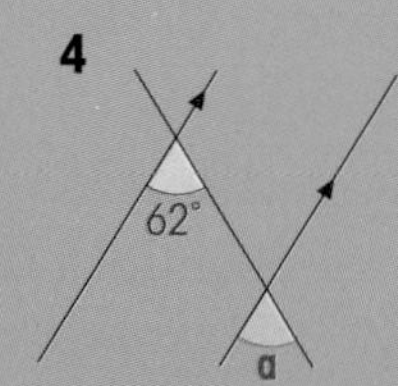

Two-dimensional shapes and three-dimensional solids

Check the facts

Two-dimensional shapes have length and width, but no depth.

Two-dimensional shapes are flat.

Examples:

Three-dimensional solids have length and width and depth.

Three-dimensional solids appear to rise out of the paper.

You can draw three-dimensional solids on isometric paper:

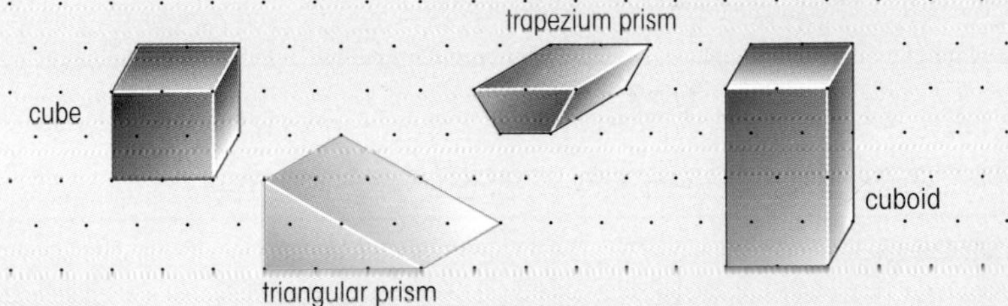

Test yourself

Copy and complete the drawings of these three-dimensional solids:

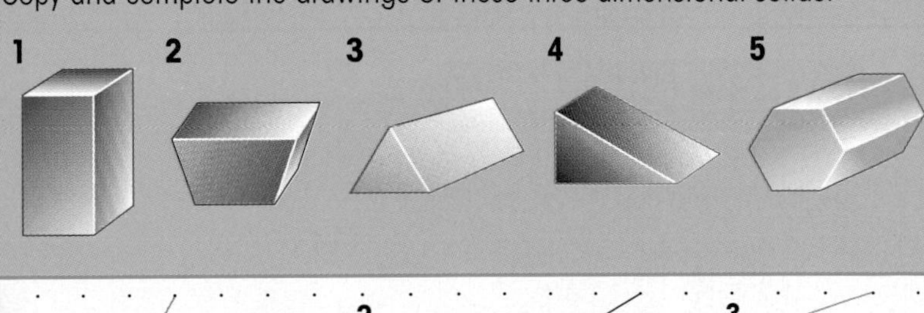

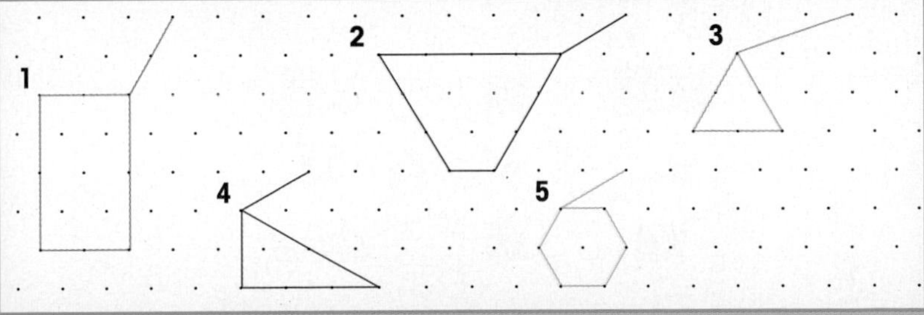

61 Two-dimensional views of three-dimensional solids

Check the facts

Three-dimensional solids have two-dimensional faces.

Look down on a three-dimensional solid and the two-dimensional shape you see is the **top elevation**.

Look at a three-dimensional solid from the front and the two-dimensional shape you see is the **front elevation**.

Look at a three-dimensional solid from the side and the two-dimensional shape you see is the **side elevation**.

Example:

This cuboid has six faces.

Four are rectangular faces and two are square faces.

The top elevation is a square.

The front and side elevations are rectangles

A **net** is a two-dimensional pattern that makes a three-dimensional solid when folded. Nets for a solid may be drawn in different ways.

Example:

This triangular prism has this net: or

Test yourself

1 Match the top, front and side elevations to the correct three-dimensional solids:

a) b) c)

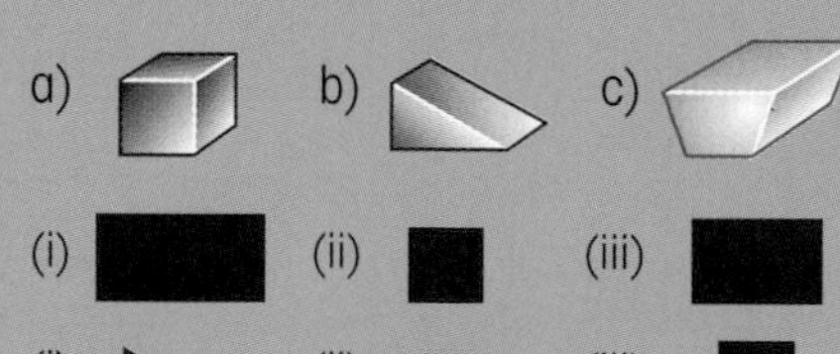

2 Draw nets of three-dimensional solids 1(a) and 1(c).

Check the facts

Polygons are closed two-dimensional shapes with straight sides. 'Closed' means all the sides join up.

Examples: These are polygons: 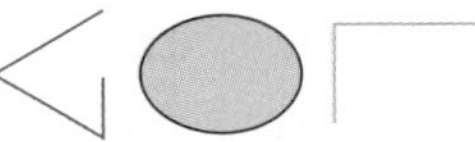

These are not polygons: 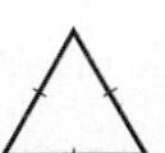

Regular polygons have all sides equal and all angles equal.
Examples: These are regular polygons:

square  equilateral triangle 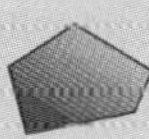

The small lines show the sides of a shape that are equal to each other.

Irregular polygons do not have all sides equal and all angles equal.
Examples: These are irregular polygons:

right-angled triangle pentagon

Note: a **pentagon** is any five-sided polygon. A **regular pentagon** has all sides equal and all angles equal. Similarly, a **hexagon** is any six-sided polygon. A **regular hexagon** has all sides equal and all angles equal.

A **quadrilateral** is any four-sided polygon.
Examples: These are quadrilaterals:   

Test yourself

Look at these labels:

not a polygon	quadrilateral	irregular polygon	regular polygon

Attach the correct label or labels to the shapes below:

1  2 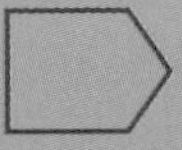 3 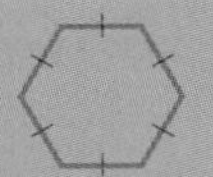 4 

5  6 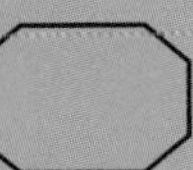 7  8

9 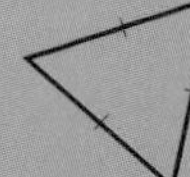 10 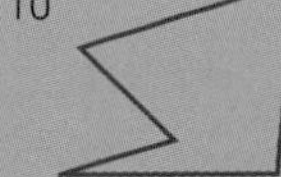 11  12 

Quadrilateral properties

Check the facts

Every quadrilateral has:
4 sides, 4 vertices (corners), 2 diagonals.

Special quadrilaterals have special properties:

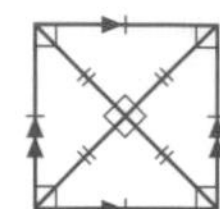

Square: a special rectangle
All sides are equal. Opposite sides are parallel.
All angles are equal. They are 90°.
Diagonals are equal. They bisect at 90°.

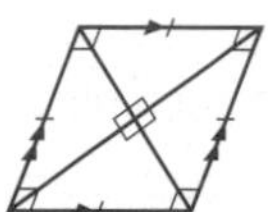

Rhombus: a squashed square
All sides are equal. Opposite sides are parallel.
Opposite angles are equal.
Diagonals are not equal. They bisect at 90°.

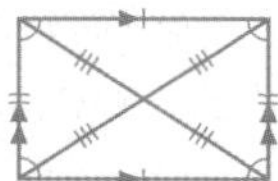

Rectangle
Opposite sides are equal and parallel.
All angles are equal. They are 90°.
Diagonals are equal.

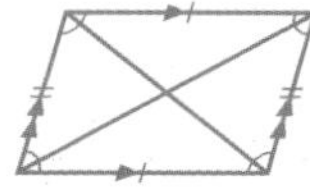

Parallelogram: a squashed rectangle
Opposite sides are equal and parallel.
Opposite angles are equal.
Diagonals are not equal.

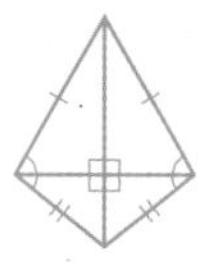

Kite: a diamond with one point longer than the other.
Sides next to each other (adjacent) are equal.
One pair of opposite angles are equal.
Diagonals are not equal. They bisect at 90°.

Trapezium
One pair of parallel sides.

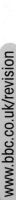

Test yourself

1 Read the statements. Which are true? Which are false?

a) A rhombus has all equal sides.
b) A kite has one pair of equal angles.
c) A parallelogram has equal diagonals.
d) A square has diagonals that bisect at 90°.
e) A rectangle has all parallel sides.
f) A trapezium has diagonals that bisect at 90°.

Check the facts

Remember: angles on a straight line add up to 180°.
(See section 58: 'Angles on a straight line and angles around a point')

Angles in a triangle also add up to 180°.

Look at these angles on a straight line:

Separate the angles:

Rearrange as a triangle:

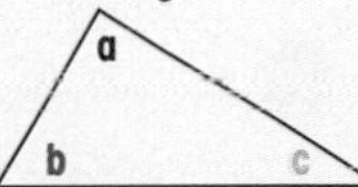

Angles **inside** vertices (corners) of polygons are called **interior angles**.
Find the sum of interior angles for polygons by looking at triangles.

Examples:

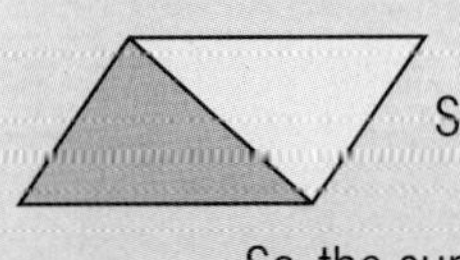

This **parallelogram** splits into two triangles.
So, the sum of interior angles = 2 × 180° = 360°.
All quadrilaterals split into two triangles.
So, the sum of interior angles for any quadrilateral = 360°.

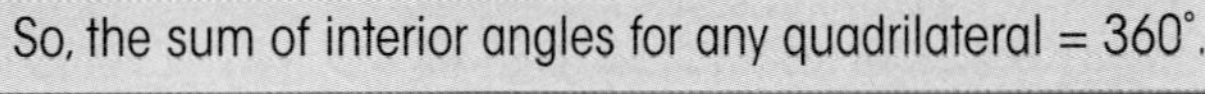

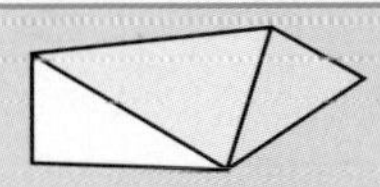

This **pentagon** splits into three triangles.
So, the sum of interior angles = 3 × 180° = 540°.

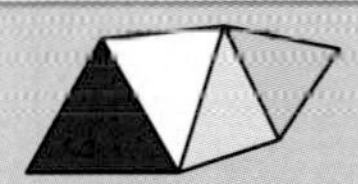

This **hexagon** splits into four triangles.
So, the sum of interior angles = 4 × 180° = 720°.

Regular polygons have equal angles.

- A regular **pentagon** has five equal angles.
  So, a regular pentagon has interior angles = 540° ÷ 5 = 108°.
- A regular **hexagon** has six equal angles.
  So, a regular hexagon has interior angles = 720° ÷ 6 = 120°.

Test yourself

You may use your calculator to help you.

1 Fill in the gaps in this table:

Shape	No. of sides	Size of interior angle
Square		
Rectangle		
Equilateral triangle		
Regular octagon		

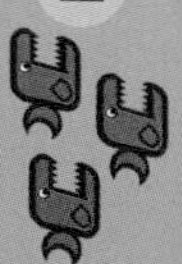

Exterior angles of polygons

Check the facts

Remember: angles around a point add up to 360° (see section 58). Angles **outside** vertices (corners) of polygons are **exterior angles**. The sum of exterior angles for any polygon is 360°.

Look at the angles around this point:

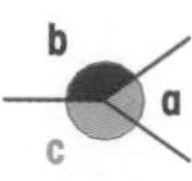

Separate the angles:

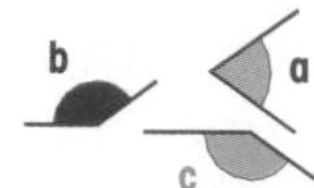

Rearrange as exterior angles of a triangle:

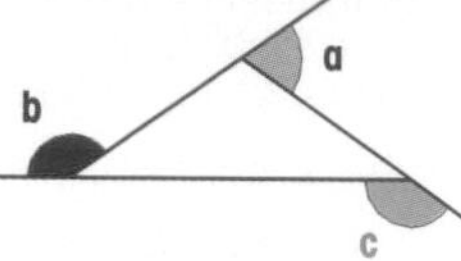

At any **vertex** (corner) of a polygon, the exterior angle and interior angle lie on a straight line.

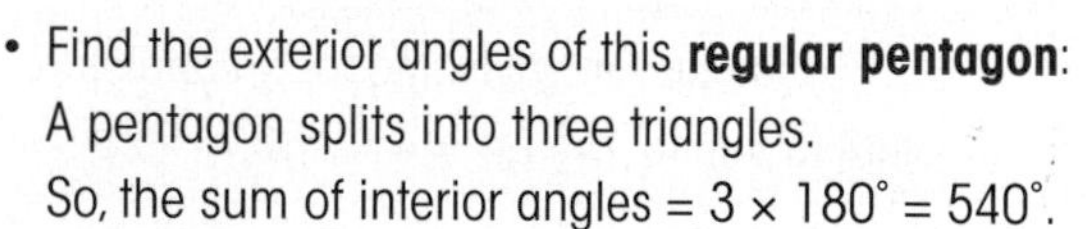

So, exterior angle + interior angle = 180°.

Examples:

- Find the missing angles in this **irregular pentagon**:

  $p = 180° - 95° = 85°$ (angles on a straight line)
  $q = 180° - 133° = 47°$ (angles on a straight line)
  $r = 180° - 127° = 53°$ (angles on a straight line)
  $s = 180° - 91° = 89°$ (angles on a straight line)
  $t = 360° - 85° - 47° - 53° - 89° = 86°$ (sum of exterior angles)

- Find the exterior angles of this **regular pentagon**:
  A pentagon splits into three triangles.
  So, the sum of interior angles = 3 × 180° = 540°.
  A regular pentagon has five equal angles.
  So, a regular pentagon has interior angles = 540° ÷ 5 = 108°.
  Exterior angle = 180° – interior angle = 180° – 108° = 72°
  (angles on a straight line).

Test yourself

You may use your calculator to help you.

1 Fill in the gaps in this table:

Shape	Size of interior angle	Size of exterior angle
Regular hexagon	120°	
Regular octagon	135°	
Regular nonagon	140°	
Regular decagon	144°	

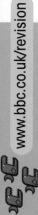

Check the facts

A circle is a set of points of equal distance from a centre.

The distance round a circle is the **circumference**:

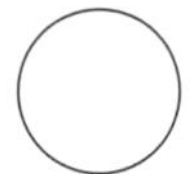

A part of the circumference is an **arc**:

The distance from the centre to the circumference is the **radius**. For this circle, radius = 1 cm.

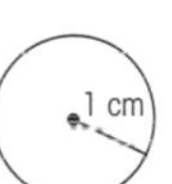

The distance from the circumference through the centre to the circumference again is the **diameter**. For this circle, diameter = 2 cm.

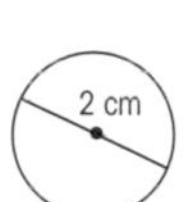

So, diameter = 2 × radius or radius = $\frac{1}{2}$ × diameter.

A **sector** is a part of a circle bounded by an arc and two radii:

Test yourself

Learn then cover the information above.

1 Now name the following parts of a circle:

a)  b)  c)  d) 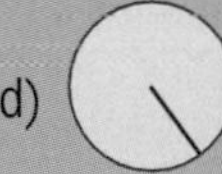 e) 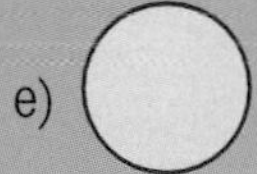

2 Calculate the diameter for each of these circles. You may use your calculator to help you.

a) 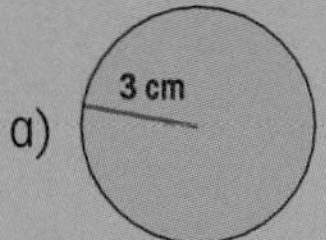

b) 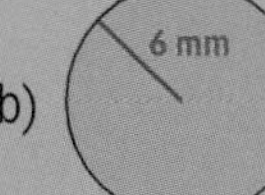

c) 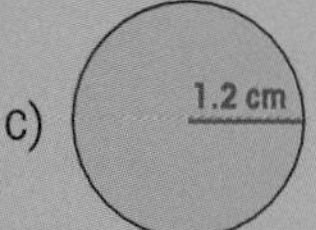

not drawn to scale

3 Calculate the radius for each of these circles. You may use your calculator to help you.

a) 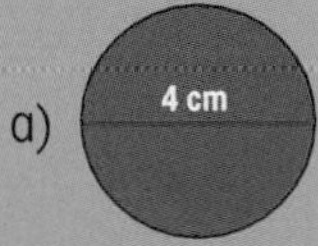

b) 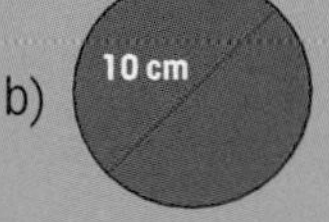

c) 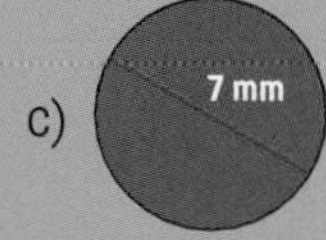

not drawn to scale

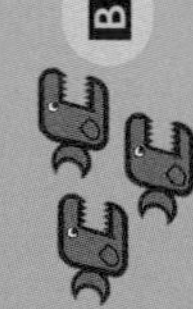

Reflective symmetry

Check the facts

A shape has **reflective symmetry** if a line can be drawn so that:

- when the shape is folded along the line, one half fits exactly over the other half
- when a mirror is placed on the line, the half shape and its reflection show the whole shape.

Examples: These shapes have **one line of symmetry**:

These shapes have **two or more lines of symmetry**:

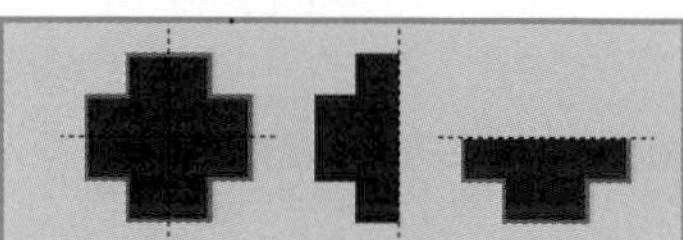
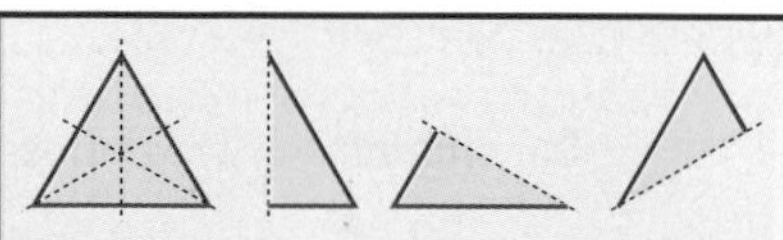

Some shapes have no lines of symmetry.

Examples:  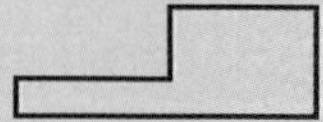 

Test yourself

Draw lines of symmetry on each of these shapes:

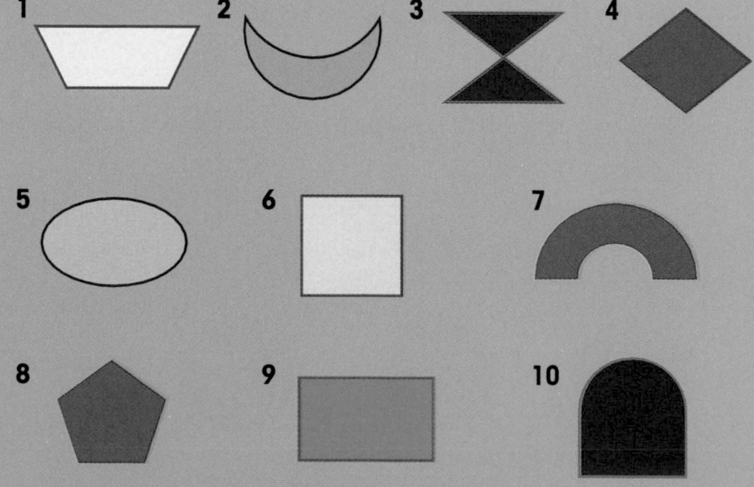

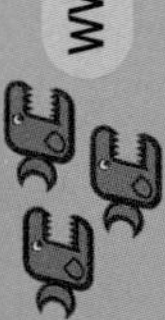

Check the facts

A shape has **rotational symmetry** if, when rotated, it looks the same in its new position.

The number of times a shape is rotated before it returns to its original position is the **order** of rotational symmetry.

Example: This shape has rotational symmetry order 2:

The circle shows the new positions of the shape. The shape rotates twice before returning to its original place.

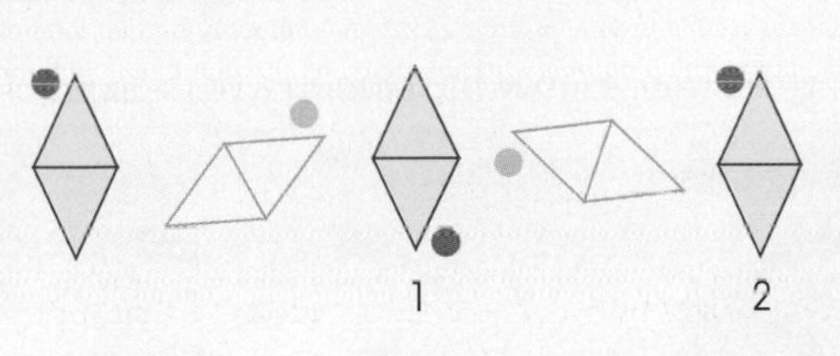

This equilateral triangle has rotational symmetry order 3:

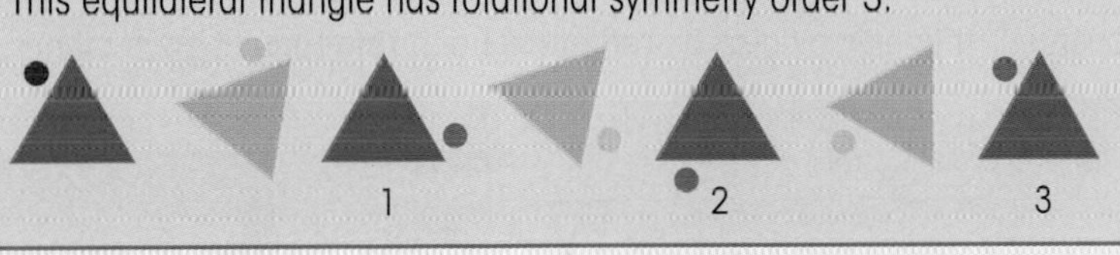

Turn the page to help you see the shapes change position.

Some shapes have no rotational symmetry. This means they have rotational symmetry order 1.

Examples: 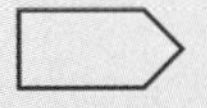  

Test yourself

1 Find the order of rotational symmetry for each of these shapes:

a)  b) 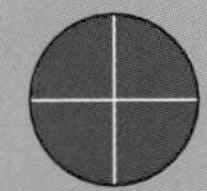 c)  d) 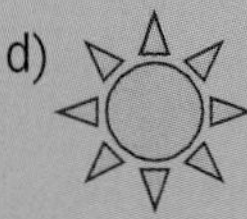

2 Find the order of rotational symmetry for each of these letters and mathematical symbols:

a) H  b) % c) ×  d) A

e) I  f) O  g) S 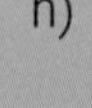 h) = 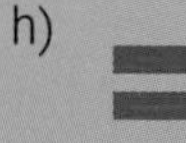

Check the facts

Shapes are **congruent** to each other if they are exactly the same size and shape.

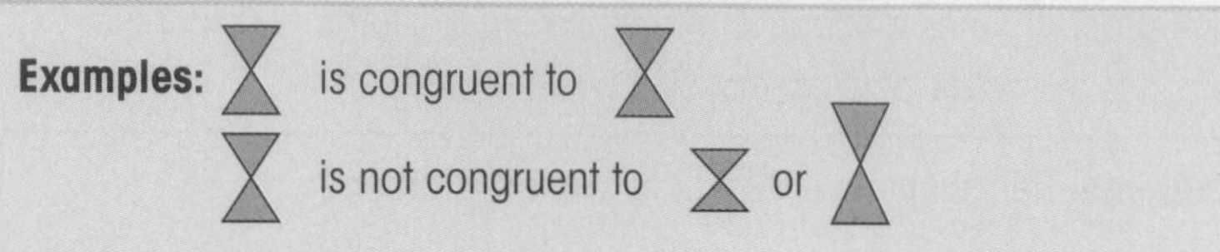

Congruent shapes may be reflections or rotations of each other.

Examples:
is a reflection of
so
is congruent to
is a rotation of
so
is congruent to

Congruent shapes may also be **reflections** and **rotations** of each other.

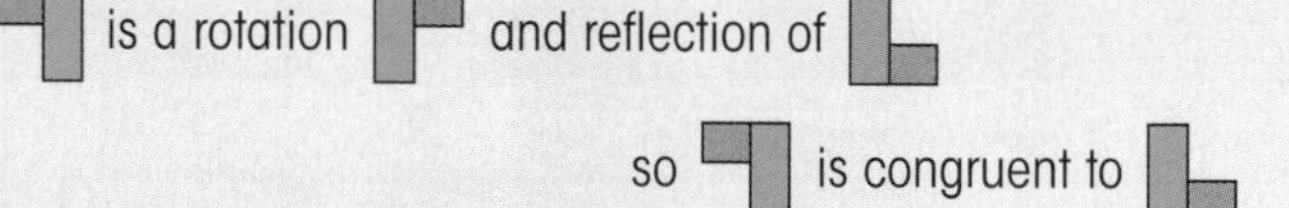

Test yourself

1 Find the five pairs of congruent tiled shapes:

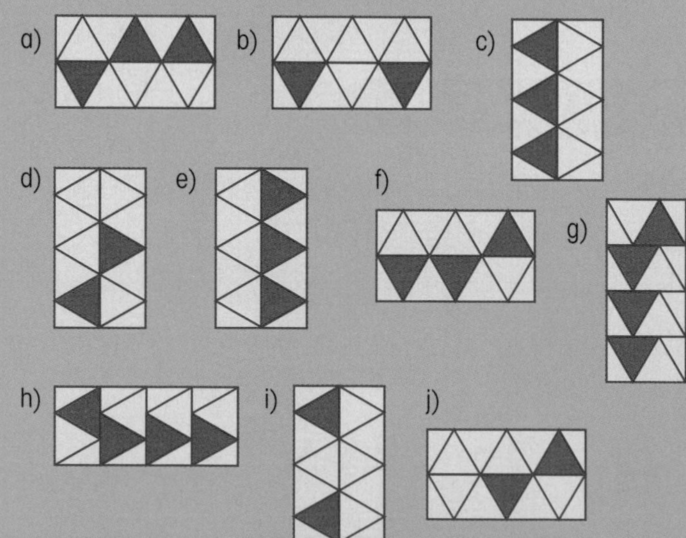

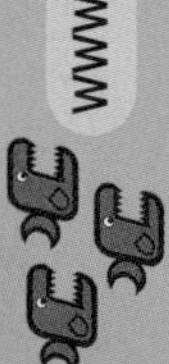

Check the facts

Shapes are **translated** if moved up ↑ or down ↓, left ← or right →.

They must remain exactly the same size and shape, with no reflection and no rotation.

Example:

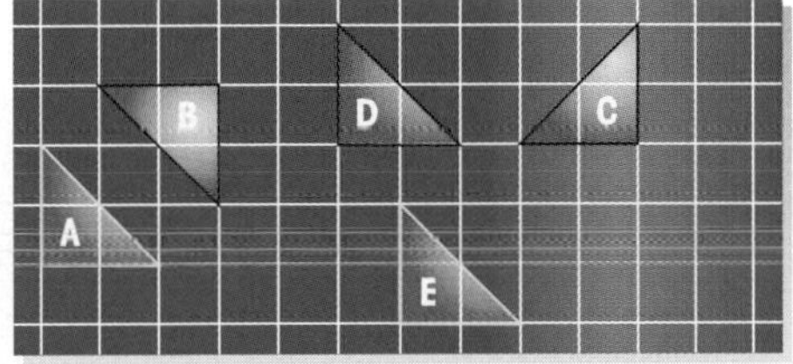

Shape B is not a translation of A because it is **reflected**.
Shape C is not a translation of A because it is **rotated**.
Shape D is a translation of A (shapes D and A are exactly the same size and shape with no reflection and no rotation).
Shape E is a translation of A (shapes E and A are exactly the same size and shape with no reflection and no rotation).

All vertices (corners) of shape A have moved five squares right and two squares up to shape D.

Shape A has been translated to shape D (5 right, 2 up).

Test yourself

1 Which shape or shapes are translations of:
a) shape P? b) shape R? c) shape X?

2 Fill in the gaps:
a) T has been translated to W (___ right, 0 down).
b) R has been translated to ___ (3 left, 2 down).
c) W has been translated to P (12 left, ___ up).
d) V has been translated to X (___ right, ___ down).
e) Q has been translated to R (3 _____, 2 _____).

Symmetry, congruence and translation

BBC KS3 Check and Test: Maths

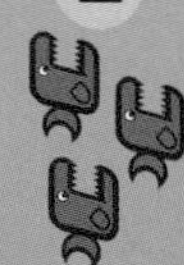

Enlargement and similar shapes

Check the facts

If a shape is **enlarged**, every side is made bigger by the same amount. That amount is called a **scale factor**.

Example:

Rectangle A is 2 units wide, 3 units long.

Enlarge rectangle A by scale factor 2.
That means multiply each side by 2.

The enlarged rectangle B is 4 units wide, 6 units long.

Enlargements of shapes do not have to be drawn the same way round.
Square X is an enlargement of Square Y by scale factor 2.

(Each side of Square X has been multiplied by 2 to make Square Y.)

Shapes are **similar** if one is an enlargement of another.

Examples: A and B are similar rectangles.
X and Y are similar squares.

Test yourself

1 Look at these shapes:

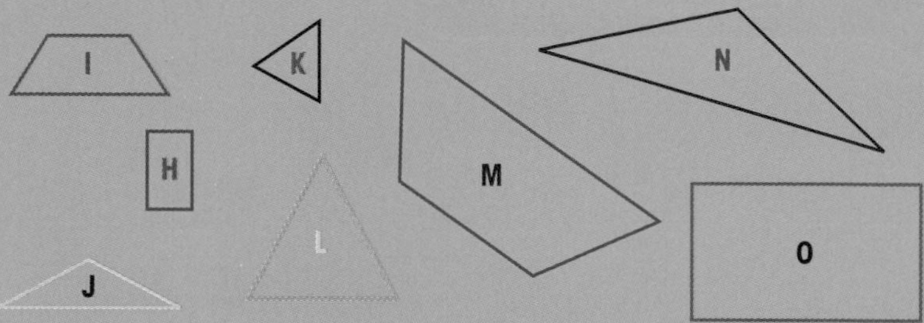

a) Which shape is an enlargement of I?
b) **L** is an enlargement of **K** by what scale factor?
c) **N** is an enlargement of **J** by what scale factor?
d) **O** is an enlargement of **H** by what scale factor?

2 Look at these shapes:

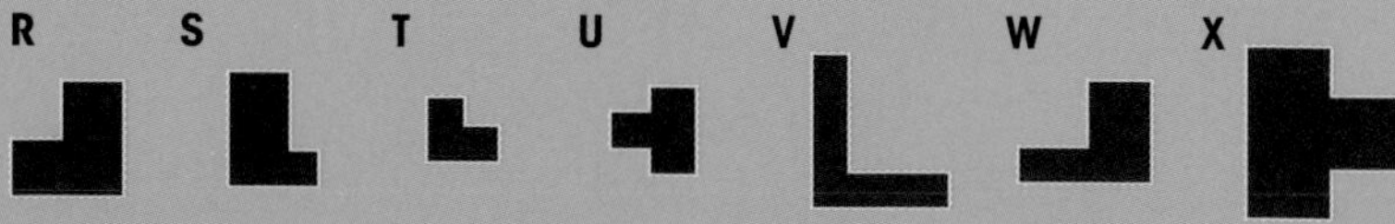

There are two pairs of similar shapes. Find the pairs.

Enlargement

www.bbc.co.uk/revision

Check the facts

To draw an enlargement you need to know the point about which to enlarge the shape. This point is called the **centre of enlargement**.

Example:

Enlarge this trapezium about point O by scale factor 3:

Draw lines from the centre of enlargement to each **vertex** (corner):

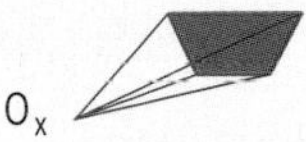

Measure each line and multiply the lengths by 3.

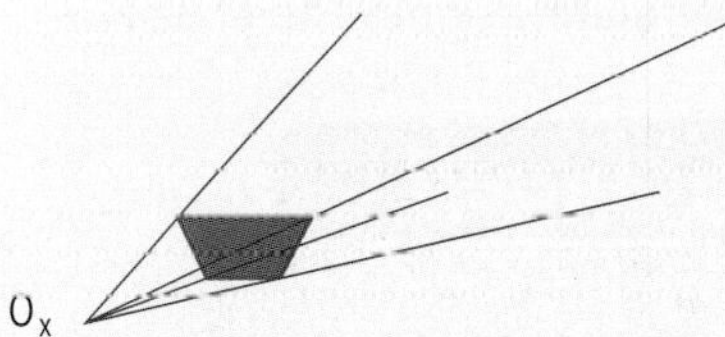

The ends of the enlarged lines mark the points of the **vertices** (corners) of the enlarged trapezium.

Join the points of the enlarged trapezium:

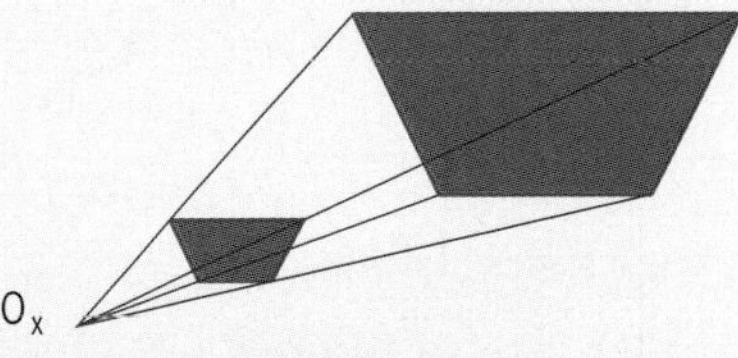

Test yourself

1 Copy and enlarge the rectangle by scale factor 2 about point A:

2 Copy and enlarge the triangle by scale factor 4 about point B:

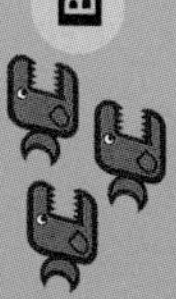

73 Units of measure

Check the facts

Metric units are the current standard units of measure.

Metric units of **length**: millimetre (mm), centimetre (cm), metre (m), kilometre (km)

Metric units of **capacity**: millilitres (ml), centilitres (cl), litres (l)

Metric units of **weight**: grams (g), kilograms (kg)

Metric units of **temperature**: degrees Celsius or centigrade (°C)

Imperial units are the old standard units of measure.

Imperial units of **length**: inches (in), feet (ft), yards (yd), miles (m)

Imperial units of **capacity**: pints (pt), gallons (gal)

Imperial units of **weight**: ounces (oz), pounds (lb), stones (st)

Imperial unit of **temperature**: degrees Fahrenheit (°F)

Test yourself

1 Look at these seven cards showing units of measure:

5 km	3 lb	4.1 °C	7 oz	1 ml	6 pints	0 °C

a) Which card shows a metric unit of temperature?
b) Which card shows a metric unit of length?
c) Which two cards show imperial units of weight?
d) Which card shows an imperial unit of capacity?
e) Which card shows an imperial unit of temperature?
f) Which card shows a metric unit of capacity?

2 Look at these eight cards showing units of measure:

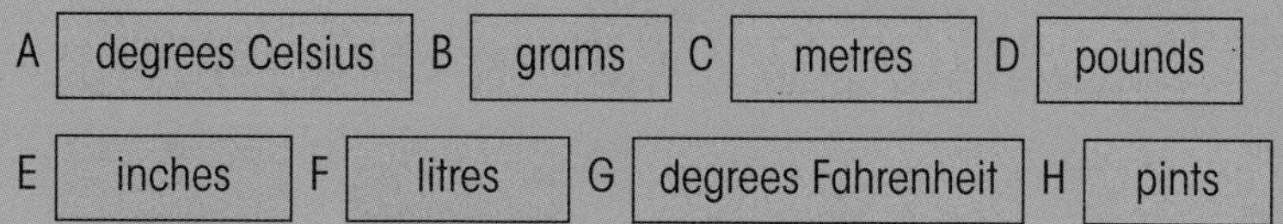

A degrees Celsius
B grams
C metres
D pounds
E inches
F litres
G degrees Fahrenheit
H pints

a) Which two cards show measures of temperature?
b) Which two cards show measures of weight?
c) Which two cards show measures of capacity?
d) Which two cards show measures of length?
e) Which four cards show metric measures?

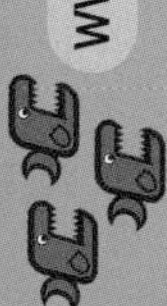

Check the facts

Metric units
Units of **length**: 10 mm = 1 cm, 100 cm = 1 m, 1000 m = 1 km
Units of **capacity**: 100 cl = 1 litre, 1000 ml = 1 litre
Units of **weight**: 1000 g = 1 kg
Note: *centi* means 100 (e.g. 100 centilitres in 1 litre)
kilo means 1000 (e.g. 1000 grams in 1 kilogram)

Imperial units
Units of **length**: 12 in = 1 ft, 3 ft = 1 yd, 1760 yd = 1 mile
Units of **capacity**: 8 pts = 1 gallon
Units of **weight**: 16 oz = 1 lb, 14 lb = 1 stone

When converting one metric unit to another or one imperial unit to another, write the conversion first. Then, if converting from a large to a small measurement, **multiply**.

Example: Change 3.2 kilometres into metres.
1 km = 1000 m, km ⟶ m is large ⟶ small
So, **multiply** by 1000: 3.2 km = 3.2 × 1000 = 3200 m

If converting from a small measurement to a large measurement, **divide**.

Example: Change 56 pints into gallons.
8 pints = 1 gallon, pints ⟶ gallons is small ⟶ large
So, **divide** by 8: 56 pints = 56 ÷ 8 = 7 gallons

Test yourself

Fill in the gaps below.
You may use a calculator.

1 The baby weighs 96 ounces. That is ______ pounds.
2 The baby is 1550 mm long. That is ______cm.
3 The girl weighs 70 lb. That is _____ stones.
4 The girl is 415 cm tall. That is ______metres.
5 The boy weighs 25 kg. That is ______g.
6 The boy is 36 inches tall. That is ______feet.
7 The adult weighs 10 stones. That is _____ pounds.
8 The adult is 1.8 m tall. That is ______cm.

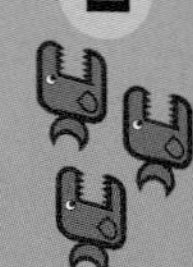

Reading scales accurately

Check the facts

Read scales accurately by looking carefully at divisions. Decide how many units each division represents.

Examples:

On this tape measure there are five 1 cm (10 mm) divisions.

Each division is 2 mm:

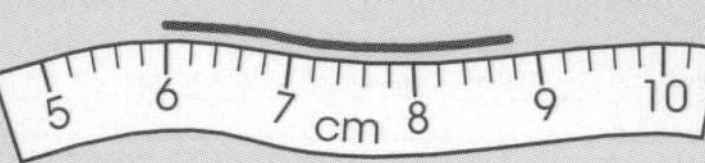

So, this piece of string is 2.8 cm long.

On this cup there are two 100 ml divisions.

Each division is 50 ml.

So, this cup contains 175 ml of water.

Test yourself

1 Look at these measuring instruments in use:

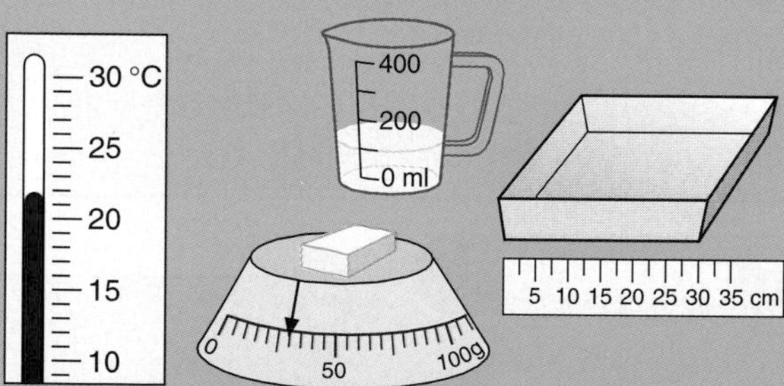

a) How many grams is each division on the scales?
b) How many millimetres is each division on the ruler?
c) How many millilitres is each division on the jug?
d) How many degrees Centigrade is each division on the thermometer?
e) How warm is the room?
f) How much does the block of butter weigh?
g) How much milk is in the jug?
h) What is the length of the baking tin?

Check the facts

Length:	1 in is about 2.5 cm 1 ft is about 30 cm	1 yd is about 90 cm 1 mile is about 1.6 km
Capacity:	1 pt is about 0.5 litres	1 gallon is about 4.5 litres
Weight:	1 oz is about 30 grams 1 lb is about 450 grams	1 stone is about 6.5 kg

When converting a metric unit to an imperial unit or vice versa, always write the conversion first.

If converting from an imperial unit to a metric unit, multiply the imperial quantity by the metric conversion value.

Example: Convert 8 oz into grams.

1 oz is about 30 g

so, 8 oz = 8 x 30 g = 240 g

If converting from a metric unit to an imperial unit, divide the metric quantity by the imperial conversion value.

Example: Convert 450 cm into yards

1 yd = 90 cm

so, 450 cm = 450 ÷ 90 yards = 5 yards

Test yourself

You may use a calculator to answer the questions below.
Look at these signs:

Oxford 10 miles

13 kg of firewood per wheelbarrow

4-litre box of wine

90 cm tall stepladders

1 Oxford is 10 miles away. How far is that in km?
2 Stepladders are sold that are 90 cm tall. How many feet is that?
3 Wine is sold in 4-litre boxes. How many pints is that?
4 13 kg of firewood is sold in a wheelbarrow. How many stones is that?

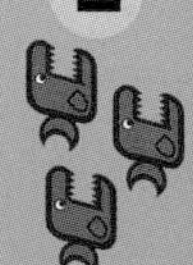

Conversion graphs

Check the facts

Sometimes conversions between units may be shown on a straight-line graph.

Example:

This graph shows the conversion from centimetres to inches and inches to centimetres.

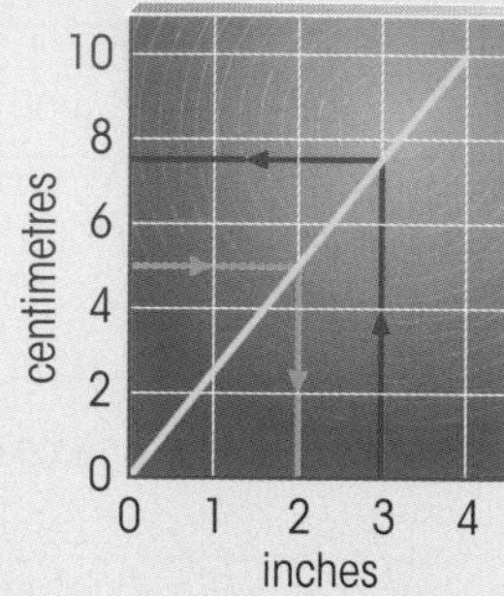

See from the graph that:

- reading across from 5 on the centimetre axis and then down to the inches axis shows that 5 cm is 2 inches
- reading up from 3 on the inches axis and then across to the cm axis shows that 3 inches is 7.5 cm.

Test yourself

Look at these two conversion graphs:

A Conversion graph of pints and litres

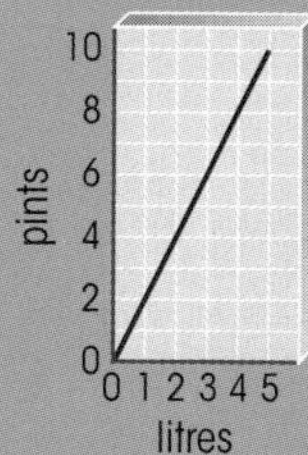

B Conversion graph of miles and kilometres

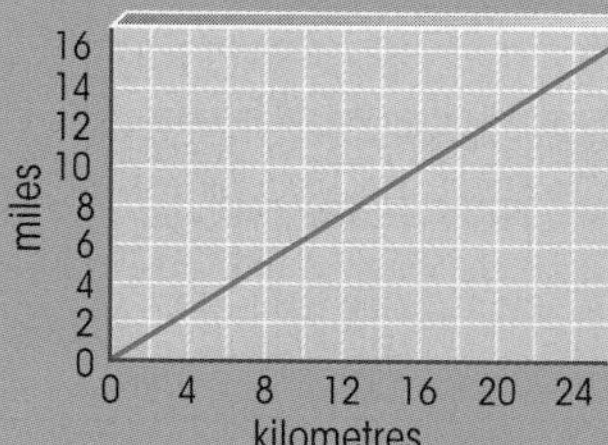

1 Use graph A to convert:

a) 6 pints to litres

b) 9 pints to litres

c) 4 litres to pints

d) 2.5 litres to pints

2 Use graph B to convert:

a) 10 miles to km

b) 8 km to miles

c) 15 miles to km

Units of measure

www.bbc.co.uk/revision

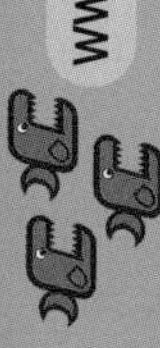

Check the facts

The perimeter of a shape is the distance all the way round the outside of that shape.

Sometimes you may wish to find the perimeter of a regular shape, such as this rectangle:

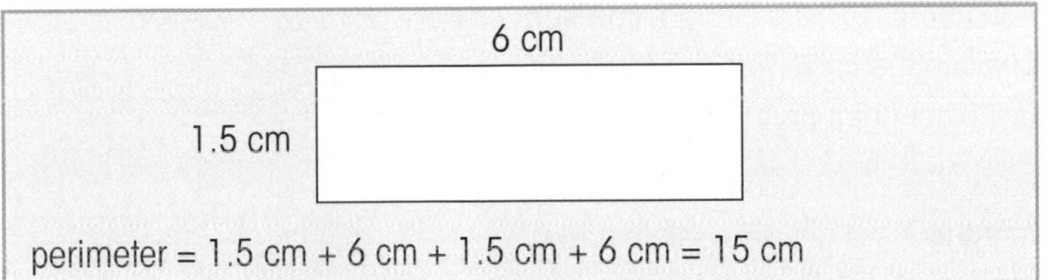

perimeter = 1.5 cm + 6 cm + 1.5 cm + 6 cm = 15 cm

Sometimes you may wish to find the perimeter of an irregular shape:

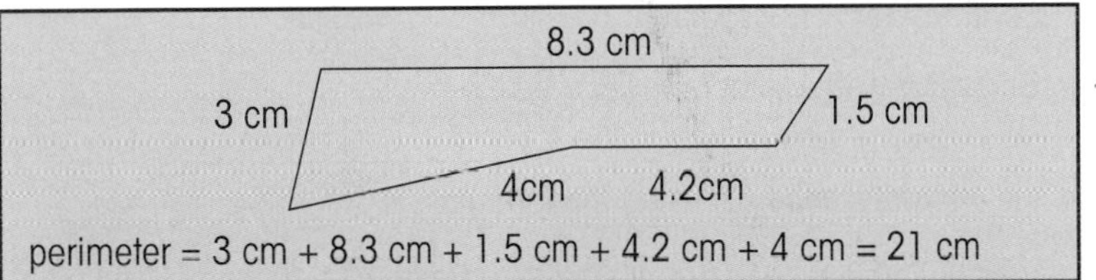

perimeter = 3 cm + 8.3 cm + 1.5 cm + 4.2 cm + 4 cm = 21 cm

Sometimes a shape is made up of smaller shapes:

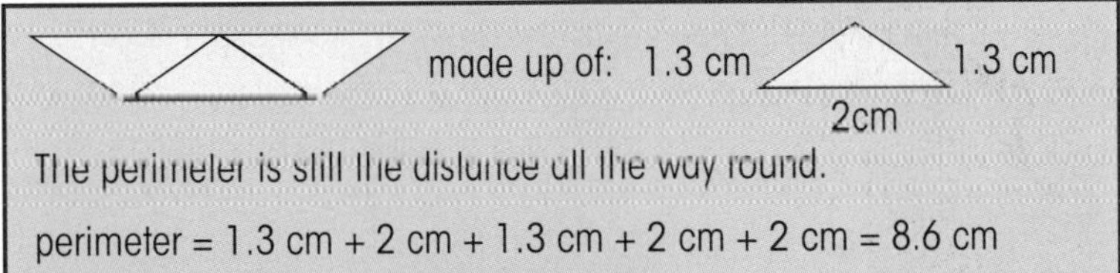

The perimeter is still the distance all the way round.

perimeter = 1.3 cm + 2 cm + 1.3 cm + 2 cm + 2 cm = 8.6 cm

Test yourself

Find the perimeters of the shapes below. You may use a calculator.

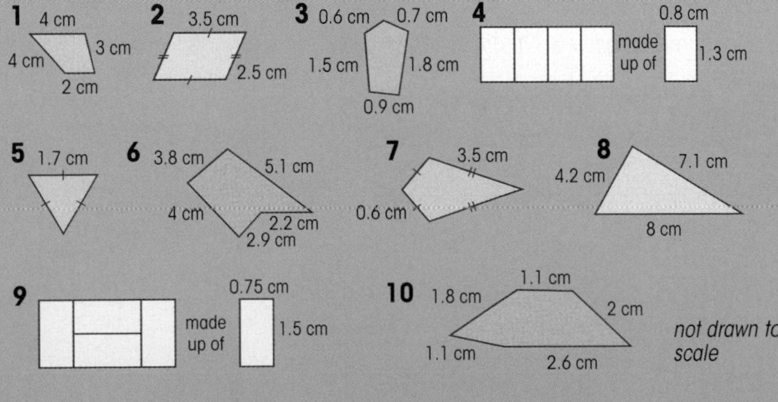

Perimeter, area and volume

BBC KS3 Check and Test: Maths

Finding the circumference of a circle

Check the facts

The perimeter of a circle is called the **circumference**.

To find the circumference of a circle you must know the **radius** or the **diameter** of the circle.

- A **diameter** (d) is a straight line from any point on the circle through the centre to any other point on the circle.

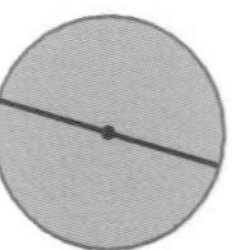

- A **radius** (r) is any straight line from a point on the circle to the centre.

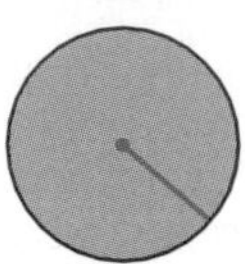

> So, **diameter** = 2 × radius, $d = 2r$
>
> Or, **radius** = diameter ÷ 2, $r = \frac{d}{2}$

Find the **circumference** (c) using the formula:

circumference = 3.14 × diameter, $c = 3.14 \times d$

or circumference = 3.14 × 2 × radius, $c = 3.14 \times 2 \times r$

Measure the circumference of a circle with string, then measure the diameter with a ruler. Now divide the circumference by the diameter and you will get an answer close to 3.14. In fact, a closer value is 3.141592653589 . . .

This decimal fraction goes on forever without repeating, so you cannot write the entire number. For this reason, the Greeks gave this number the name pi, π.

So, **circumference = π × diameter or π × 2 × radius**

Example:

diameter = 4 cm

so, circumference = 3.14 × 4 = 12.56 cm

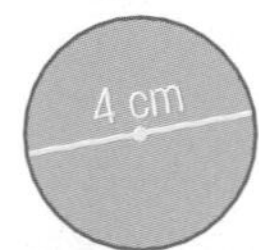

Test yourself

Find the circumference of these circles. You may use a calculator.

1

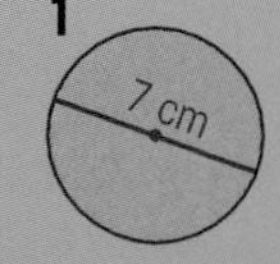

2

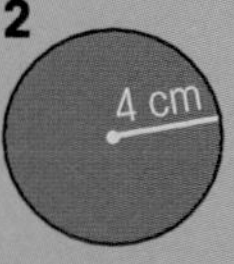

3

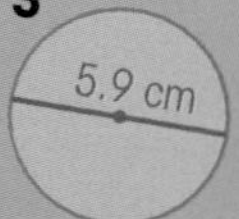

4

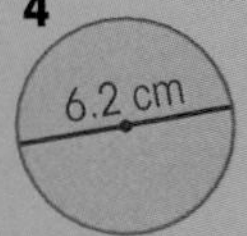

5

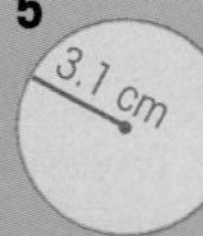

6

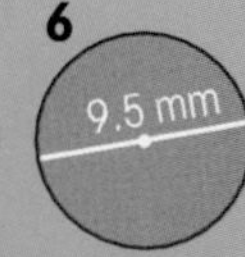

Check the facts

The **area** of a two-dimensional shape measures the amount of space that the shape covers.

Units of area are called **square units**. They may be mm^2 (millimetre squared), cm^2 (centimetre squared), m^2 (metre squared) or km^2 (kilometre squared).

This is 1 cm^2 

This is 2 cm^2  = 

This is 3 cm^2 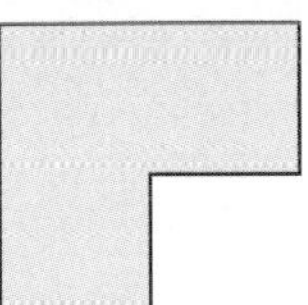 = 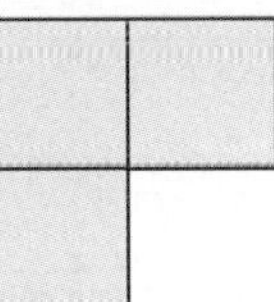

You can find areas by counting unit squares.

Example:

The area of this Y-shape is 5 units squared.

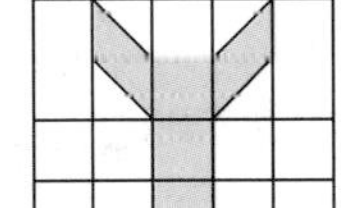

(3 × ▢ and 4 × ◹)
Notice that ◹ is half ▢ so, 2 × ◹ = ▢

Test yourself

Find the areas of the red shapes below:

1 

2 

3 

4 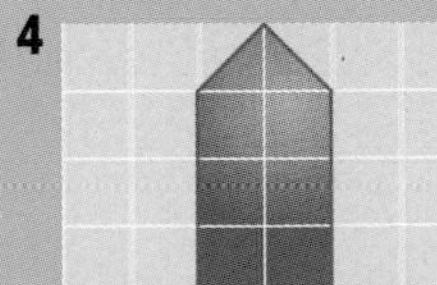

5 

6 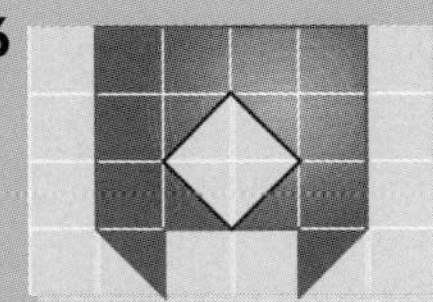

Using formulae to find area

Check the facts

Areas of regular shapes can be found using **formulae**.

Look at this **square**: 

It is 2 units long and 2 units wide. Area = 4 units squared.
The area of a square = length × length.

Look at this **rectangle**: 

It is 3 units long and 2 units wide. Area = 6 units squared.
The area of a rectangle = length × width.

Look at this right-angled triangle: 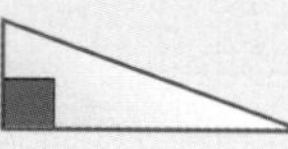

It is half a rectangle: 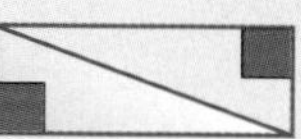

So, the area of a **right-angled triangle** = $\frac{1}{2}$ × length × height.

Area of any **triangle**: 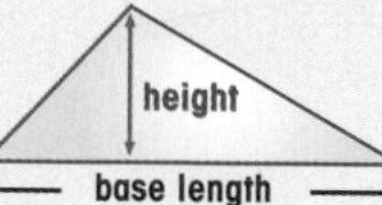

= $\frac{1}{2}$ × base length × height

Area of a **parallelogram**: 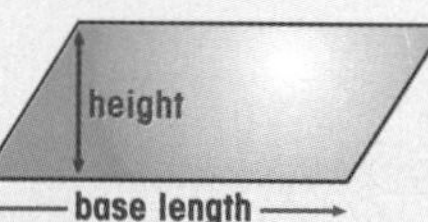

= base length × height

Area of a **trapezium**: 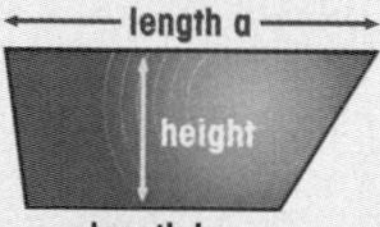

= $\frac{1}{2}$ (length **a** + length **b**) × height

Test yourself

Find the area of the shapes below. You may use a calculator.
not drawn to scale

1 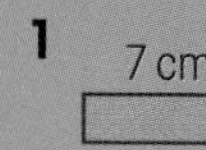

2 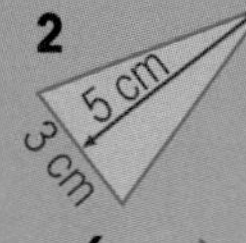

3 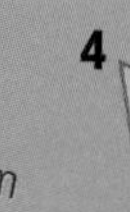

4 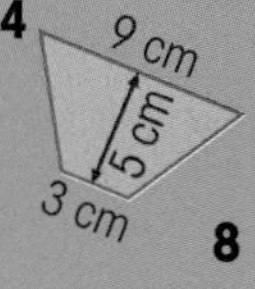

5 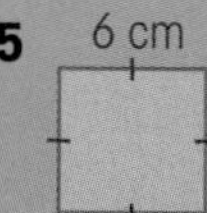

6 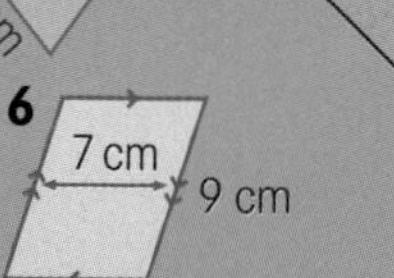

7
7 cm
6 cm

8
0.6 cm
1.5 cm
3.4 cm

Perimeter, area and volume

www.bbc.co.uk/revision

Check the facts

The area of a circle is $\pi \times$ **radius** $\times$ **radius**

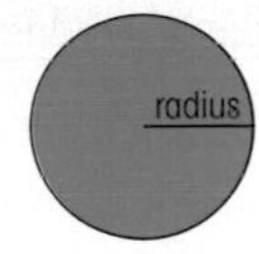

Remember, π (pi) is a name given to the number 3.141592653589 . . .

Round π to 3.14

Area of a circle = 3.14 × radius × radius

If asked for an **approximation**, round π **to 3**.

Approximate area of a circle = **3** × **radius** × **radius**

Examples:

Find the area of these circles:

A

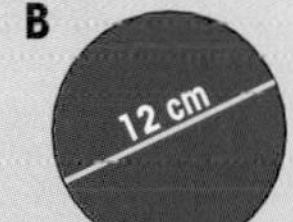

B

12 cm

Area of A $= 3.14 \times \text{radius} \times \text{radius}$

$= 3.14 \times 5 \times 5 = 78.5 \text{ cm}^2$

Area of B $= 3.14 \times \text{radius} \times \text{radius}$

(**Remember**: radius = diameter ÷ 2 = 12 ÷ 2 = 6 cm)

$= 3.14 \times 6 \times 6 = 113.04 \text{ cm}^2$

Test yourself

1 Find the area of the circles below. You may use a calculator.

a)

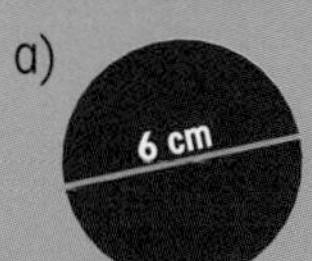

b)

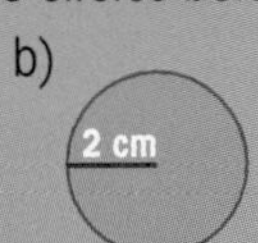

c)

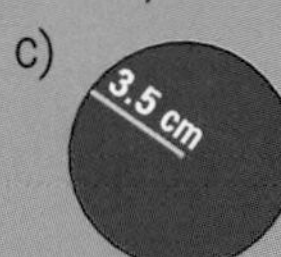

Remember: circumference of a circle = 3.14 × diameter
area of a circle = 3.14 × radius × radius.
Don't confuse these formulae!

2 Find the circumference and area of each circle below. You may use a calculator.

a)

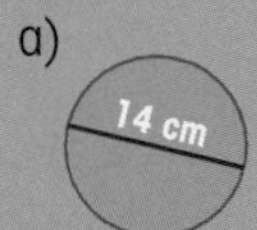

b)

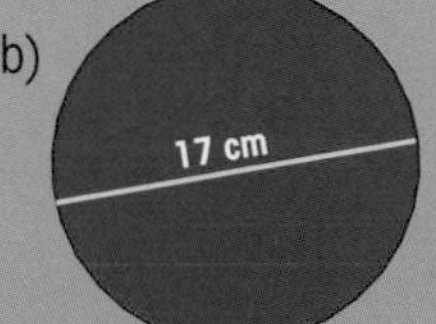

c)

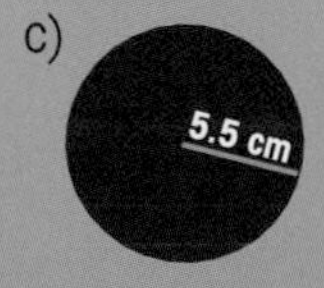

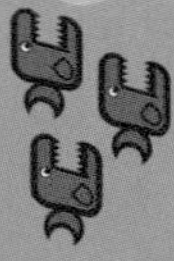

What is volume?

Check the facts

The **volume** of a three-dimensional solid measures the amount of space that the solid takes up.

The units of volume are called **cubic units** and may be **mm³** (millimetre cubed), **cm³** (centimetre cubed), **m³** (metre cubed) or **km³** (kilometre cubed).

This is 1 cm³

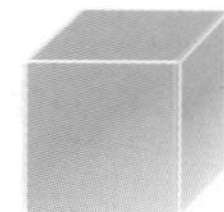

This is 2 cm³

=

This is 3 cm³

=

You can find volumes by counting unit cubes.

Example:

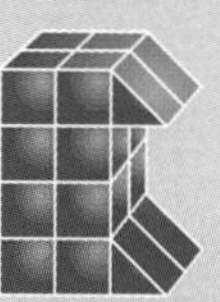

The volume of this solid is 18 units cubed.

(16 × 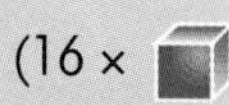 and 4 × 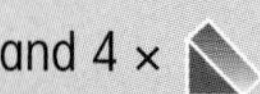)

Notice that  is half  so, 2 × ◣ = ▣

Test yourself

Find the volumes of these solids:

1

2

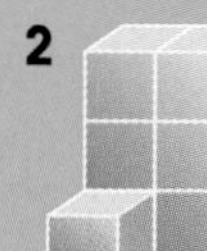

3

4

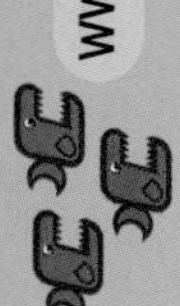

Using formulae to find volume

Check the facts

Volumes of solids can be found using formulae.

- Look at this cube:

It is 2 units long and 2 units wide and 2 units high.
volume = 8 units cubed

The volume of a cube = length × length × length.

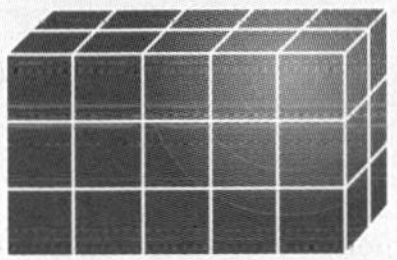

- Look at this cuboid:

It is 5 units long and 2 units wide and 3 units high.
volume = 30 units cubed

The volume of a cuboid = length × width × length.

(It does not matter which length you call 'length', 'width' and 'height'. The order of multiplication does not alter an answer.
$5 \times 2 \times 3 = 2 \times 5 \times 3 = 2 \times 3 \times 5 = 30$ units cubed)

Example: Find the volume of this cube:

volume = $3 \times 3 \times 3 = 27\ \text{cm}^3$

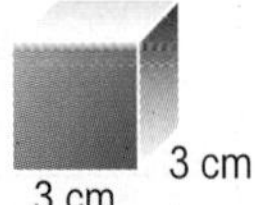

Test yourself

You may use your calculator to help you.

Find the volumes of these solids.

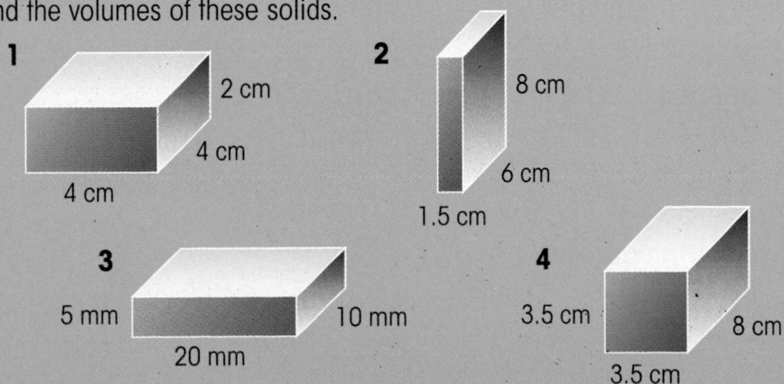

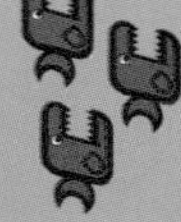

85 Finding loci

Check the facts

A **locus** is a path of points that follow a rule.

A locus of points that is always at the same distance from point x makes a circular path.

- Here is x:
- Now mark points 0.5 cm from x in every direction:

- The result is a circle:

A locus of points always at the same distance from points A and B makes a straight-line path.

- Here are points A and B. Now mark points equal distances from A and B in every direction: A B
- The result is a straight line: A B

A locus of points that is always at the same distance from a line AB makes a path of two straight lines parallel to AB and two semicircles at points A and B.

- Here is the straight line AB. Now mark points 5 mm from AB in every direction:

- The result is this path: A B

Test yourself

1 Rover the dog is tied to a post P on a 1 m lead. Rover runs round the post with his lead stretched at 1 m. What is the locus of Rover's path? (1 cm to represent 1 m)

.P

2 a) Kate jogs along a canal towpath always at a distance of 0.8 m from the canal. Draw the locus of Kate's jog along the towpath. (1 cm to represent 1m)

canal

b) Kate then jogs home through a park on a path that is equal distance from a bench B and a football post F. Draw the locus of Kate's jog through the park.

B· ·F

Loci

www.bbc.co.uk/revision

Check the facts

Data that is collected but is not put in any order is called **raw data**. You can order this data using a **frequency chart**.

A frequency chart tallies quantities. Tallies are bundled in fives.

Examples: / 1 // 2 /// 3 ~~////~~ 5 ~~////~~ // 7 ~~////~~ ~~////~~ 10

In a frequency chart, each tally is totalled and written as a number (the frequency).

Example: There are six pitches for tents at Osney campsite. The number of tents pitched at Osney campsite each Saturday night from April to September is as follows:

0 1 0 0 2 5 5 4 6 5 6 6 6 5 4 6 6 5 3 6 5 3 0 1 1 0

number of tents	tally	frequency
0	~~////~~	5
1	///	3
2	/	1
3	//	2
4	//	2
5	~~////~~ /	6
6	~~////~~ //	7

Test yourself

Cornhead Local Library conducted a survey of 30 people to find out:

1 a) The kind of books people like

type of books	tally	frequency
fiction	~~////~~ ~~////~~ /	11
biography	//	
cookery	~~////~~ /	
gardening		8
arts		3

b) The days people like to visit the library

days	tally	frequency
Mon	//	2
Tue		7
Wed		0
Thu	~~////~~	
Fri	////	
Sat		12

Complete the missing tallies and frequencies in the frequency tables.

2 These are the number of books people tend to borrow:

1 3 0 2 4 1 5 2 2 3 4 2 2 2 4

5 2 4 1 1 2 3 2 5 4 3 2 1 2 2

Draw a frequency table for this data.

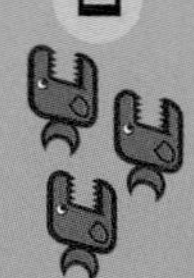

Grouped data

Check the facts

Large amounts of data spread over a large range may be grouped.

Example: There are 30 pitches for caravans at Osney campsite. The number of caravans pitched at the campsite each Friday and Saturday night from May to August is as follows:

3	1	2	4	2	7	3	6	6	6	11	14	9
8	10	6	12	11	13	21	25	26	29	20	28	19
23	27	28	30	25	30	28	28	26	26	24	30	23
25	23	26	27	25	29	28	19	19	8	10	2	5

The number of caravans pitched range from 0 to 30. This is a large range, so you can order the information into class intervals. As a general rule, choose class intervals so that the frequency table has between 5 and 10 class intervals.

no. of caravans	tally	frequency
1–5	~~////~~ //	8
6–10	~~////~~ ~~////~~	10
11–15	~~////~~	5
16–20	////	4
21–25	~~////~~ ////	9
26–30	~~////~~ ~~////~~ ~~////~~ /	16

This frequency table has six class intervals.

Test yourself

1 The number of books returned late to Cornhead local library each day it is open for the month of March is as follows:

6	1	3	10	4	5	15	8	3	23	4
9	8	7	11	5	7	2	4	19	11	

Group this data and draw the frequency table:

number of books	tally	frequency

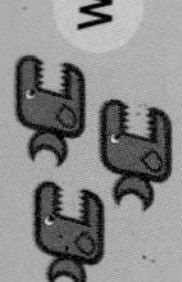

Check the facts

You may display frequency chart data on a **bar chart**.

Example: The number of cars at Osney campsite each Saturday night from April to September is as follows:

no. of cars	tally	frequency (f)
1–3	/	1
4–7	~~////~~ ///	8
8–10	~~////~~ ~~////~~ ////	14
11–14	//	2
15–17	/	1

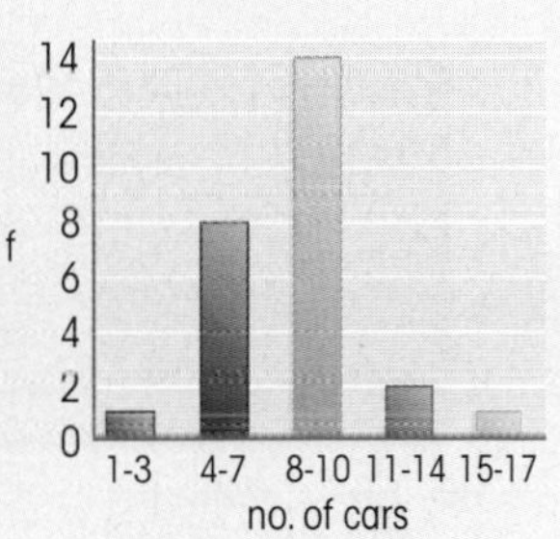

Notice that the bar chart has a title, labelled axes, bars of equal width and bar lengths the same as frequencies.

Test yourself

1 Cornhead Fitness Centre surveyed visitors to find out what activity they most often came to do.

a) Which activity was the most popular?

b) How many people came to the fitness centre to swim?

c) How many people were surveyed altogether?

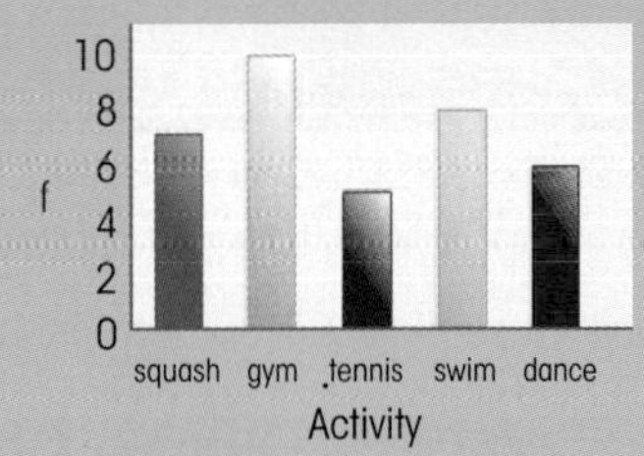

2 Cornhead Fitness Centre also surveyed visitors to find out how long they tended to spend at the centre in a visit. Display this data in a bar chart.

time	tally	frequency (f)
0–30 mins	///	3
30–60 mins	~~////~~	5
$1–1\frac{1}{2}$ hrs	~~////~~ ~~////~~	10
$1\frac{1}{2}–2$ hrs	~~////~~ ~~////~~ ///	13
more than 2 hrs	////	4

Drawing and interpreting line graphs

Check the facts

Line graphs may be used to display all kinds of data.

Examples:

- Line graphs may be used to show sales. Here are the sales of tickets on an open-top bus tour for a week in May:

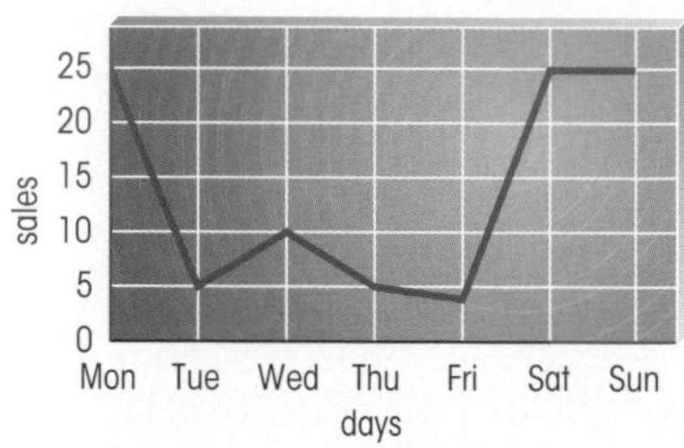

Graphs tell stories. Notice that there are as many sales on Monday as Saturday and Sunday, suggesting Monday was perhaps a bank holiday.

- Line graphs may be used to show journeys. Here are the journeys to work of Jeremy and Elaine. Jeremy travels by car and Elaine travels by bus.

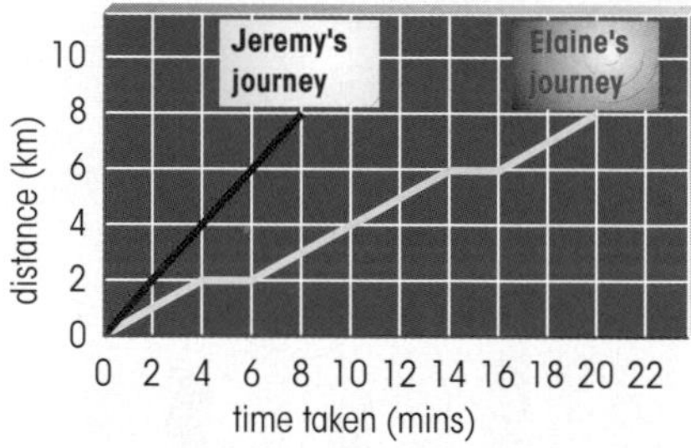

Graphs tell stories. Notice the steps in the graph of Elaine's journey. The horizontal lines of the steps show when the bus stopped.

Look again at section 77 for more line graphs.

Test yourself

Rick, Rob and Ron ran a 1500-metre race, shown on this graph:

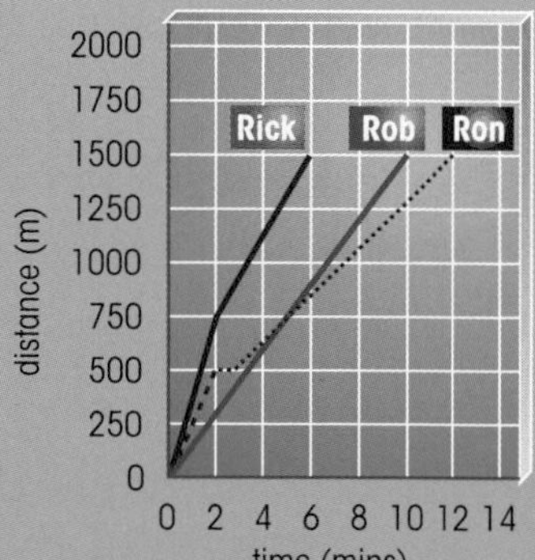

1 Who was fastest at the start?

2 Ron stopped during the race. Why do you think this was?

3 At what time into the race did Rob overtake Ron?

4 Rick did not see where the race ended and ran for a further 500 m. This took him 2 minutes. Show this on the graph.

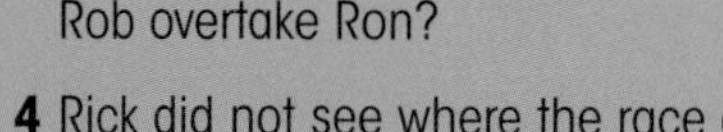

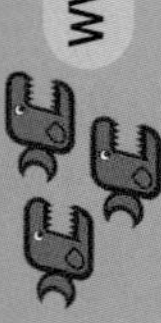

Check the facts

Data may be displayed in **pie charts**. A pie chart is a diagram that looks like a circular pie that has been cut into **sectors** (portions). The data is represented by the whole circular pie and each quantity is represented by a sector of the circle.

Example:

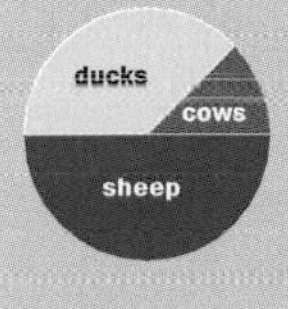

This pie chart shows animals on Shifrin Farm.

$\frac{1}{8}$ sector shows the proportion of cows

$\frac{3}{8}$ sector shows the proportion of ducks

$\frac{1}{2}$ sector shows the proportion of sheep

To interpret pie charts, you need to understand fractions.

(Look again at section 29: 'Calculating fractions of whole numbers'.)

Example: Look at the pie chart above.

If the farmer has 160 animals on the farm, then

the $\frac{1}{8}$ sector (showing the proportion of cows) represents

$\frac{1}{8}$ of $160 = 160 \div 8 = 20$ cows

the $\frac{3}{8}$ sector (showing the proportion of ducks) represents

$\frac{3}{8}$ of $160 = 3 \times \frac{1}{8}$ of $160 = 3 \times 20 = 60$ ducks

the $\frac{1}{2}$ sector (showing the proportion of sheep) represents

$\frac{1}{2}$ of $160 = 160 \div 2 = 80$ sheep

Test yourself

You may use a calculator to help you.

1 The pie chart shows the shoe sizes of Year 9 students at Burtle School. The there are 216 students in Year 9.

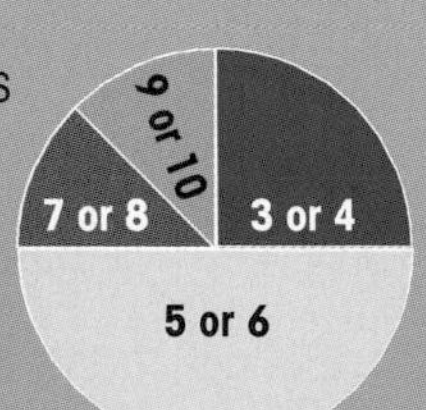

a) $\frac{1}{6}$ of the students wear size 7 or 8 shoes.
How many students wear size 7 or 8 shoes?

b) $\frac{1}{12}$ of the students wear size 9 or 10 shoes.
How many students wear size 9 or 10 shoes?

c) What fraction of Year 9 wear size 3 or 4 shoes?

d) How many students wear size 3 or 4 shoes?

e) What fraction of Year 9 wear size 5 or 6 shoes?

f) How many students wear size 5 or 6 shoes?

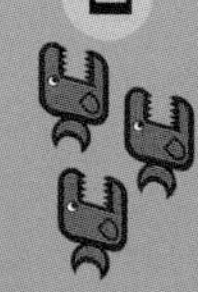

Mode

Check the facts

Mode is a type of average.

The mode is the most **popular quantity**.

Example: At Shifrin Farm Shop the number of boxes of eggs that have been sold is counted at the end of each week. The numbers of boxes sold at the end of each week from April to June were:
16 10 17 18 14 15 18 17 16 18 19 20 18.

When finding the mode, it helps to order quantities by size:
10 14 15 16 16 17 17 18 18 18 18 19 20.

Mode (the most popular quantity) = 18 boxes of eggs
(18 boxes was the most popular quantity sold in a week)

This is the data in a bar chart:
Notice that when data is displayed in a bar chart, the mode is the tallest bar.

So mode = 18 boxes of eggs

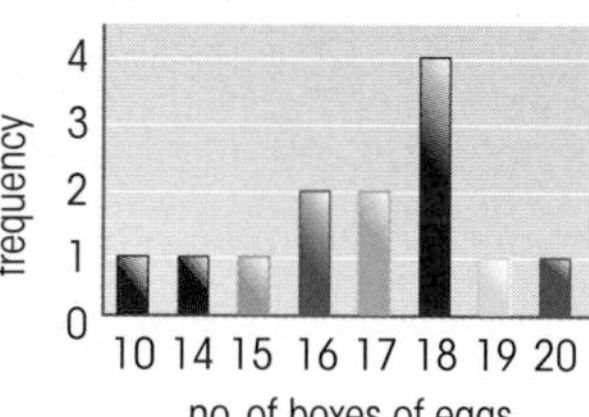

Test yourself

1 A factory counts the number of chocolates in boxes that it produces. Find the modal number of chocolates for *Cheerful Chocs, Chocs in Blocks* and *Posh Chocs*:

a) The contents of 11 boxes of *Cheerful Chocs*:
23, 25, 21, 23, 22, 23, 22, 24, 23, 21, 24

b) The contents of 10 boxes of *Chocs in Blocks*:
12, 13, 12, 12, 11, 13, 15, 12, 14, 13

c) The contents of 15 boxes of *Posh Chocs*:
7, 6, 6, 8, 6, 6, 8, 6, 6, 7, 7, 6, 8, 7, 8

2 These bar charts show the shoe size of students in two different classes. Find the modal shoe size in each class.

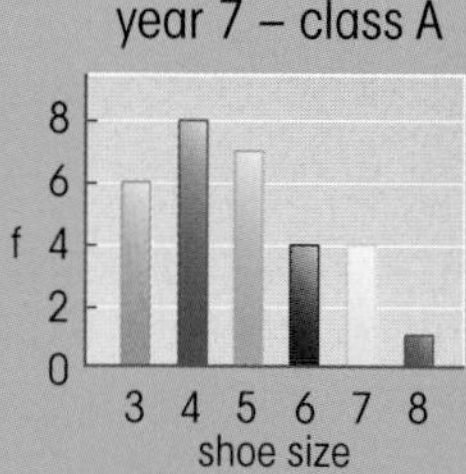

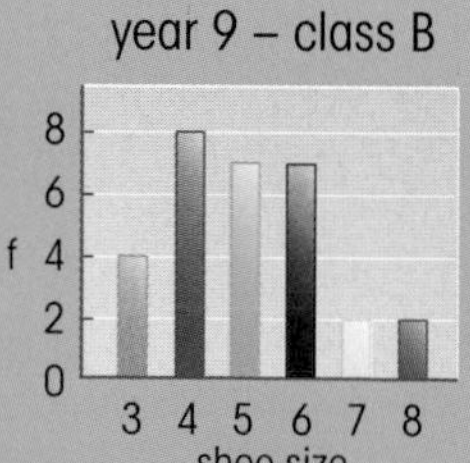

Check the facts

Median is a type of average.

The median is the **middle quantity** when all quantities are placed in size order.

Example:
The number of onions sold at Shifrin Farm Shop is counted each day. Here are the results for the week 11th to 18th April: 12 9 8 3 6 5 9.

- Order quantities by size: 3 5 6 8 9 9 12
  There are seven quantities, so the **middle quantity** is the 4th:
  3 5 6 (8) 9 9 12
  median (the middle quantity) = **8 onions**
- Onion sales are counted for a further week:
  3 5 7 8 9 9 12 10 0 4 6 8 4 3
  Order the quantities: 0 3 3 4 4 5 6 7 8 8 9 9 10 12
  There are 14 quantities, so the **middle quantities** are the 7th and 8th:
  0 3 3 4 4 5 (6 7) 8 8 9 9 10 12
- When there are two middle quantities, the **median** falls halfway between them. Halfway between 6 and 7 is 6.5.
  median (the middle quantity) = 6.5 onions

Test yourself

1 A factory counts the number of people working on production lines a, b and c for a week. Find the median number of people working on each line:
a) 19, 17, 19, 18, 16, 17, 17
b) 9, 8, 8, 9, 10, 7, 9
c) 21, 23, 21, 22, 22, 22, 20.

2 A factory counts the number of boxes of chocolates coming off its production lines a, b and c every five minutes for half an hour. Find the median number of boxes of chocolates coming off each production line:
a) 14, 10, 15, 13, 14, 15
b) 10, 8, 8, 11, 10, 2
c) 12, 11, 13, 11, 11, 13.

Mean and range

Check the facts

Mean is a type of average.

The mean is the **total of all quantities** divided by **the number of quantities**.

Example: At Shifrin Farm Shop the number of pallets of strawberries sold is counted at the end of each week for the nine weeks of June and July. Here are the results:

20 24 8 10 13 19 20 10 11

To find the **mean**, add all quantities:

20 + 24 + 8 + 10 + 13 + 19 + 20 + 10 + 11 = 135

Now divide by the number of quantities, that is 9:

mean = 135 ÷ 9 = 15 pallets of strawberries

The farm manager looks at last year's sales results, collected for eight weeks from the beginning of June. He calculates, mean = 16.75.

It is not possible to sell 0.75 of a pallet, so round to the nearest pallet: mean = 17 (to the nearest pallet).

The range can help you understand an average.

range = largest value – smallest value

For last year's strawberry pallet sales, range = 24 – 8 = 16.

For this year's strawberry pallet sales, range = 18 – 14 = 4.

The range shows that sales did not vary as much this year as last year. Perhaps this was because of regular advertising last year.

Test yourself

Freda has a choice of four tube lines to take to work: red, blue, green or brown. Freda travels on each line for one week. She records how many minutes late the tube arrives at her stop each day. Here are the results:

Red: 5, 2, 5, 6, 5 Blue: 8, 2, 9, 0, 1

Green: 12, 11, 8, 10, 9 Brown: 11, 1, 0, 16, 0

1 Calculate the **mean** number of minutes late for each line.

2 Find the **range** of number of minutes late for each line.

3 Which tube line should Freda take? Give a reason for your answer.

Check the facts

Scatter diagrams allow you to compare two sets of data at the same time.

Example: For two weeks, a survey was conducted to find out how temperature affects the use of facilities in Ravens Park. At midday, park staff counted the number of people using the facilities and measured the air temperature.

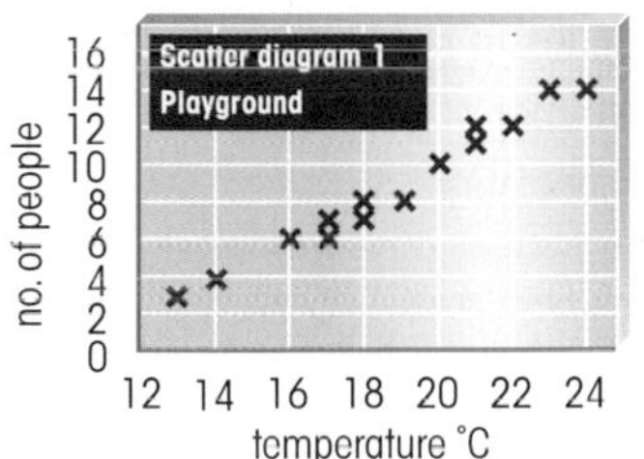

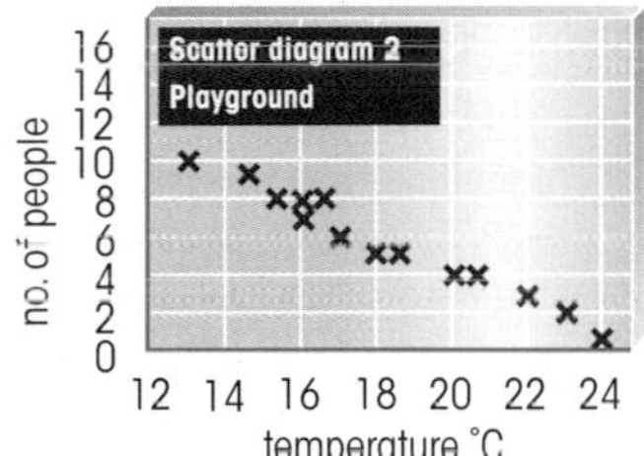

Scatter diagram 1 shows that as the temperature increases, the number of people in the playground increases.

> If one variable increases as the other increases, it is called **positive correlation**.

Scatter diagram 2 shows that as the temperature increases, the number of people in the gallery falls.

> If one variable increases as the other decreases, it is called **negative correlation**.

Test yourself

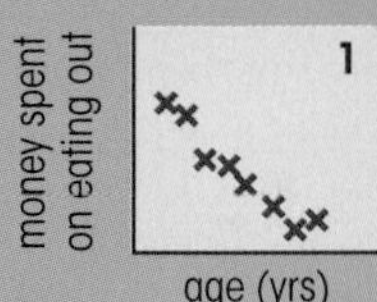

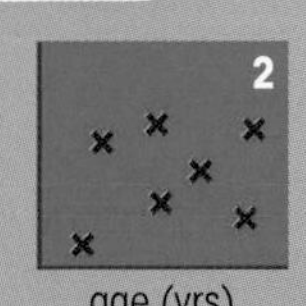

Look at the scatter diagrams and fill in the gaps below with one of the words:

increases	decreases	positive	negative	no

Diagram 1 shows that as age (a)________, amount of money spent on eating out (b)________. This is (c)________correlation.

Diagram 2 shows that there is (a)________ correlation between a person's age and the money spent on clothes.

Diagram 3 shows that as age (a)________, amount of savings in the bank (b)________. This is (c)________ correlation.

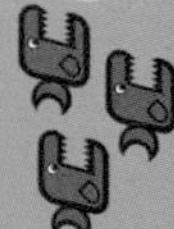

Drawing a line of best fit

Check the facts

If a scatter diagram shows some correlation between two variables, then a straight-line graph can be drawn to represent the relationship between the two variables. This line is called the **line of best fit**. Draw a line of best fit so that it goes through as many points on the scatter diagram as possible, with close to an equal number of points on either side of the line.

Example: Ravens Park conducted a survey for two weeks to find out how temperature affects the use of facilities in the park. At midday each day, park staff counted the number of people using facilities and measured the air temperature.

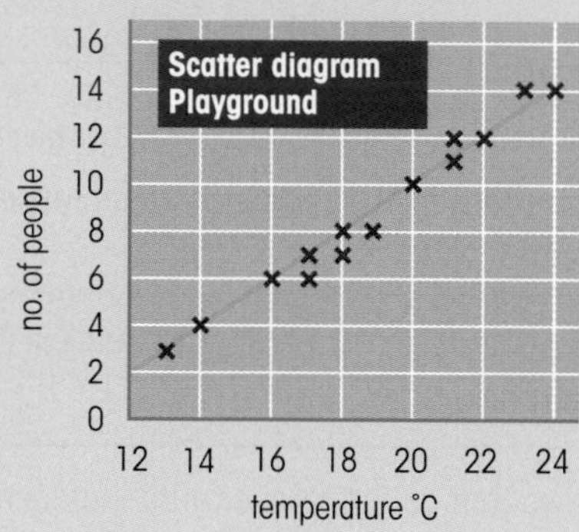

This line of best fit goes through nine points, with three points on one side of the line and two points on the other. From the line, you can see at 15 °C Ravens Park can expect five people in the playground.

Test yourself

1 This scatter diagram shows the results of a maths test and a science test for a Year 9 class. Draw a line of best fit on the scatter diagram.

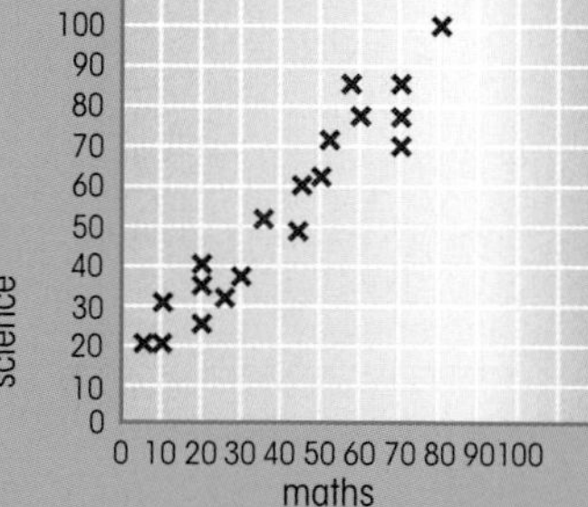

2 a) Ed was absent for the science test, but scored 50% in his maths test. What mark would you expect him to get in his science test?
b) Flo was absent for the maths test, but scored 75% in her science test. What mark would you expect her to get in her maths test?

Check the facts

Probability measures chance.

Chance can be described in words: **impossible** **certain** **unlikely** **evens** **very likely** **likely** **very unlikely**

These words can be written on a scale:

impossible — very unlikely — unlikely — evens — likely — very likely — certain

These words describe how likely it is that there will be a particular outcome to an event.

- An **event** is something that happens, say a coin being flipped or a card being picked.
- An **outcome** is the result of an event, say a head being called when a coin is flipped or a Queen of Hearts being chosen when a card is picked.

Probability is the number that shows the chance of a particular outcome of an event. Probability is measured as a fraction between 0 and 1.

> An **impossible** event has an outcome of probability 0.
>
> A **certain** event has an outcome of probability 1.
>
> An **evens** statement has an outcome of probability $\frac{1}{2}$.

Test yourself

1 Read these statements. Place each statement letter on the scale of chance.

A When I toss this coin, it will land on tails.

B Pigs will fly.

C It will snow in May.

D Tuesday will come after Monday next week.

E There will be a soap opera on TV at 7.30 pm tonight.

impossible — unlikely — evens — likely — certain

2 Look at these spinners: spinner 1 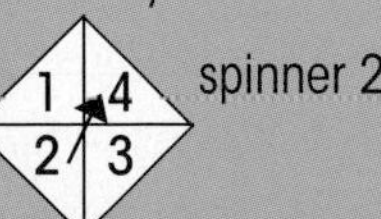

spinner 2 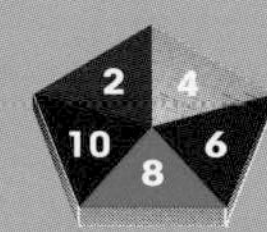

a) Which spinner gives the best chance to get an even number?

b) Which spinner gives the best chance to get a 2?

c) What is the probability of getting an odd number on spinner 2?

Probability

BBC KS3 Check and Test: Maths

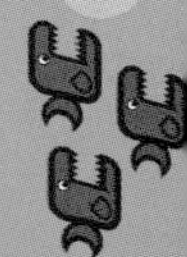

Calculating probability

Check the facts

The probability (or chance) of an outcome to an event can be calculated using this formula:

$$\textbf{P (outcome)} = \frac{\textbf{number of favourable outcomes}}{\textbf{number of all possible outcomes}}$$

Example: Look at this scale:

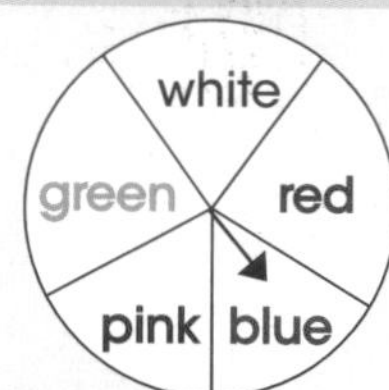

- What is the probability of getting blue?
  Blue is a favourable outcome.
  There is one **favourable** outcome.
  There are five **possible** outcomes.

$$\text{P (outcome)} = \frac{\text{number of favourable outcomes}}{\text{number of all possible outcomes}} = \frac{1}{5}$$

- What is the probability of getting red, pink or white?
  Red, pink or white are favourable outcomes.
  There are three favourable outcomes.
  There are five possible outcomes.

$$\text{P (outcome)} = \frac{\text{number of favourable outcomes}}{\text{number of all possible outcomes}} = \frac{3}{5}$$

Test yourself

1 a) Andrea asks Phil to guess in which month her birthday is. What is the probability that Phil makes a correct guess?
b) Phil guesses June. This is incorrect. What is the probability that Phil makes a correct guess now?
c) Andrea's birthday is in December. What is the probability that Andrea's birthday is Christmas Eve or Christmas Day?

2 In a quiz, contestants must choose envelope A, B, C or D.

A History questions	**B** Sports questions	**C** Music questions	**D** Sports questions

a) What is the probability of choosing envelope A?
b) What is the probability of choosing envelope's B, C or D?
c) Sian chooses an envelope. What is the probability of Sian getting sports questions?
d) Sian chooses envelope C. It cannot be used again. Now Paul chooses an envelope. What is the probability of Paul getting sports questions?

Check the facts

You will need to use mental methods in all three Key Stage 3 test papers. Mental methods are like maths 'tricks'. They will save you work!

One mental method is to use known facts to find out unknown facts.

Example: Here is part of the 35 times table:

$1 \times 35 = 35$
$2 \times 35 = 70$
$3 \times 35 = 105$
$4 \times 35 = 140$

Use the 35 times table to calculate 35 x 6.
One way to do this is:

$35 \times 6 = (35 \times 4) + (35 \times 2) = 140 + 70 = 210$

Use the 35 times table to calculate 35×8.
One way to do this is: $35 \times 8 = (35 \times 4) \times 2 = 140 \times 2 = 280$

Another mental method that will help you is to use your head to check whether an answer is sensible.

Example: A rectangular field is 29.8 m long and 21.7 m wide.
Without using a calculator, pick out the area of the field: 6059.66 m^2 or 401.56 m^2 or 646.66 m^2 .
The area of the field must be 646.66 m^2
(because 29.8 m is about 30 m and 21.7 m is about 20 m
area of rectangle = length $\times$ width
so, area of rectangular field is about $30 \times 20 = 600$ m^2).

Test yourself

1 This is part of a conversion table:
This conversion table is used by sailors.
It converts miles into nautical kilometres.

50 miles = 92.6 km
100 miles = 185.2 km
150 miles = 277.8 km

Use the conversion table to answer these questions:
a) How far is 200 miles in nautical kilometres?
b) How far is 350 miles in nautical kilometres?

2 Mrs Goulbourn buys five items at the shopping centre.
They cost £6.99, £2.98, £25.99, £67.75 and 95p.
Without using a calculator, pick out Mrs Goulbourn's total bill:
£100.36 or £104.66 or £98.85.

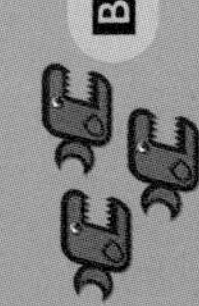

Preparing for a mental maths test: Tier 3–5

Check the facts

You will need to prepare for your mental maths test. The only way to do this is practice.

The test below is a lower-tier test for those taking **Tier 3–5** papers. It should take 10 minutes. Work out the answers in your head and write them on a piece of paper. You are only allowed to use pens and pencils.

Test yourself

Ask a friend or parent to read the questions below. They should read each question twice and then give you the correct amount of time to answer it.

For these questions, you will have 5 seconds to write your answer.

1 A room is 400 cm long. How many metres is that?

2 Divide fifty-six by eight.

3 What number do you add to thirty-six to make fifty?

4 How many degrees are there in half a right angle?

For these questions, you will have 10 seconds to write your answer.

5 The time is 20:23. How many minutes is this before nine o'clock in the evening?

6 A square has sides of 8 cm. What is its perimeter?

7 14% of a class play a musical instrument. What percentage do not play a musical instrument?

8 Write down the expression, $2y + y + 3y$. Now simplify it.

9 A city has a population of five million one thousand six hundred and forty-two. Write this number in figures.

10 Multiply nine by seventy.

11 Write down the expression, $7p - q$. What is its value when p is five and q is eight?

For these questions, you will have 15 seconds to write your answer.

12 A milkman sells a pint of milk for twenty-four pence. How many pints will Mrs Norman get for one pound?

13 There are sixty pupils in a school play. There are twice as many girls as boys. How many girls are there?

14 You buy three items in a shop. One costs 99p, another costs 30p and another costs 20p. How much change do you get from £1.50?

15 In a game of chance, four balls are put in a bag: two red balls, a green ball and a blue ball. A ball is taken out of the bag at random. What is the probability that this ball is red?

Check the facts

You will need to prepare for your mental maths test. The only way to do this is practice.

The test below is a lower-tier test for those taking **Tier 4–6** papers. It should take 10 minutes. Work out the answers in your head and write them on a piece of paper. You are only allowed to use pens and pencils.

Test yourself

Ask a friend or parent to read the questions below. They should read each question twice and then give you the correct amount of time to answer it.

For these questions, you will have 5 seconds to write your answer.

1. Add the numbers 10, 5 and 3. Now find a third of their total.
2. Write the number 346.1 to the nearest 10.
3. How many centimetres are in 14 metres?
4. The probability that I get a 2 on a spinner is one fifth. What is the probability that I do not get a 2?

For these questions, you will have 10 seconds to write your answer.

5. 20% of a number is 6. What is the number?
6. Angle *s* and angle *t* lie on a straight line. Angle *s* measures 72°. What does angle *t* measure?
7. Write down the expression $3x - 1$. Find its value when x equals 8.
8. What is 640 minus 83?
9. The fraction of boys in an athletic club is $\frac{3}{7}$. What fraction of the club are girls?
10. x stands for a number. Write an expression for the following: multiply x by 5, then subtract 3 from the result.
11. Work out 0.03 multiplied by 9.

For these questions, you will have 15 seconds to write your answer.

12. Write down these weights: 5 g, 7 g, 11 g, 6 g, 5 g. Underline the median length.
13. You get 880 yen for four pounds. How many yen do you get for two pounds?
14. A cuboid is 4 cm long, 3 cm wide and 5 cm high. What is its volume?
15. A large plate has circumference 90 centimetres. Approximately what is its diameter?

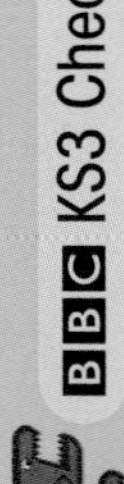

Answers

01 Place value

1 a) 7 b) 1 c) 0
2 a) 4601 b) 12 057
3 a) 1506 or 1507 b) 8765

02 Adding and subtracting

1 a) 20 b) 7 c) 29
d) 87 e) 91 f) 38
2 a) 5749 b) 3832 c) 1987
3 100 kg – 43 kg = 57 kg

03 Multiplying

1 a) 24 b) 40 c) 63 d) 42
e) 32 f) 56
2 a) 5046 b) 1138 c) 22 991
d) 43 960 e) 4619 f) 140 712

04 Dividing

1 a) 6 b) 6 c) 8 d) 5 e) 6 f) 7
2 a) 78 b) 384 c) 973 d) 21
e) 33 f) 67

05 Word problems

1 a) 21 b) 1959 c) 56
2 a) 6 b) £151.80 c) £6.60

06 Factors and multiples

1 a) 1, 3, 5, 15
b) 1, 2, 4, 7, 14, 28
c) 1, 2, 3, 4, 6, 8, 12, 24
d) 1, 5, 7, 35 e) 5 f) 4
2 a) 36, 30, 72, 60, 18
b) 36, 30, 72, 60, 18
c) 36, 27, 72, 18
d) 30, 60 e) 18 f) 30

07 Prime, square and cube numbers

1 a) 23 b) 2 c) 36 d) 64 e) 81

08 Powers and square roots

1 a) 16 b) 27 c) 81
2 a) 5^4 b) 7^5 c) 10^4 d) 3^7
3 a) 10 b) 7 c) 6 d) 4 e) 2 f) 9
g) 8 h) 5

09 Multiplying by 10, 100 and 1000

1 a) 240 b) 700 c) 9000 d) 3500
e) 820 f) 4000
2 a) 100 b) 100 c) 10 d) 1000
e) 100 f) 1000

10 Dividing by 10, 100 and 1000

1 a) 36 b) 330 c) 9 d) 505
e) 20 f) 330
2 a) 10 b) 10 c) 100 d) 1000
e) 100 f) 100
3 £450

11 Multiplying and dividing by multiples of 10, 100 and 1000

1 a) 6000 b) 25 000 c) 24 000
d) 12 000 e) 30 f) 300
g) 45 000 h) 400 i) 1800
2 a) 40 b) 20 c) 600 d) 1500
e) 50 f) 20
3 £18

12 What is a negative number?

1 a) smaller b) smaller c) bigger
d) bigger
2 a) –6, –2, –1, 5, 7, 8
b) –10, –7, –3, 0, 2, 9
3 –18 °C, –11 °C, –3 °C, –1 °C, 3 °C, 15 °C

13 Adding and subtracting with negative numbers

1 a) –2 b) 3 c) –8 d) 1
e) 17 f) –5
2 a) 6 b) 7 c) –10
3 a) 3 °C b) 6 °C c) 13 °C

14 Multiplying and dividing with negative numbers

1 a) –28 b) –9 c) 4 d) –12 e) –5
f) 36 g) –6 h) 6 i) –56
2 –2 and 3
3 –3 and –4
4 –4

15 The BODMAS rule

1 a) 15 b) 18 c) 30 d) 45
e) 15 f) –1
2 a) 48 b) 4 c) 8 d) 70
3 a) 4 × 2 + 5 b) 7 + 3 × 2
c) 8 × 3 – 4 d) 10 × 3 ÷ 6

16 Using a calculator

1 a) 1 b) 15 c) 8
2 a) 1024 b) 13 c) 19 d) 18
e) 324 f) –16 g) 343 h) 150
i) 140

3 a) $6 \div 3 \times 9 - 4 = 14$
b) $9 \times 4 \div 6 - 3 = 3$
c) $6 \div 3 \times 4 - 9 = -1$

17 What is a decimal?

1 a) 1 b) 7 c) 0 d) 8
2 a) 271.40 b) 92.3 c) 408.06
d) 0.19
3 a) £4.30 b) £51.09 c) £0.08

18 Ordering decimals

1 a) smaller
b) smaller
c) bigger
d) smaller
2 a) 4.005, 4.05, 4.1
b) 0.09, 0.62, 0.8
c) 7.77, 7.779, 7.78
d) 0.63, 6.34, 63.4
e) 91.5, 91.56, 91.6
f) 309.02, 309.2, 309.21
g) 5.108, 5.67, 5.9
h) 23.61, 23.6611, 32.16

19 Rounding decimals

1 a) 8.9 b) 62.8 c) 0.6 d) 35.8
e) 92.5 f) 107.7 g) 0.7 h) 241.7
2 a) 67.93 b) 4.50 c) 0.03
d) 82.11 e) 19.19 f) 1.30
3 a) 5829.249 b) 0.208 c) 3.142
d) 29.481 e) 9.277 f) 2.400

20 Adding and subtracting decimals

1 a) 28.57 b) 56.4 c) 27.12
d) 153.78 e) 21 f) 41.73
g) 301.62 h) 136.87 i) 503.11
2 a) £28.13 b) £37.04 c) £7.04
d) £137.84

21 Multiplying and dividing decimals by single-digit whole numbers

1 a) 60.88 b) 406.6 c) 2.38
d) 12.86 e) 5.58 f) 64.78
g) 105.8 h) 241.16 i) 4183.28
2 a) £85.50 b) £8.45

22 Multiplying and dividing decimals by 10 and 100

1 a) 0.467 b) 5.61 c) 7780
d) 0.6081 e) 0.034 f) 70
2 a) 100 b) 100 c) 100 d) 10
e) 100 f) 10

23 What is a fraction?

1 a) $\frac{3}{5}$ shaded
$\frac{2}{5}$ not shaded
b) $\frac{5}{8}$ shaded
$\frac{3}{8}$ not shaded
c) $\frac{3}{10}$ shaded
$\frac{7}{10}$ not shaded
2 a) b) c) d)

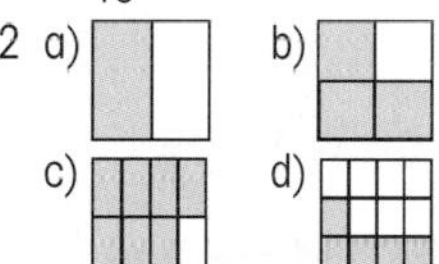

24 Equivalent fractions

1 a) $\frac{4}{20}$ b) $\frac{5}{20}$ c) $\frac{2}{20}$ d) $\frac{15}{20}$ e) $\frac{14}{20}$
2 a) $\frac{14}{24}$ b) $\frac{16}{24}$ c) $\frac{20}{24}$ d) $\frac{18}{24}$ e) $\frac{12}{24}$
3 a) $\frac{2}{9}$ b) $\frac{2}{5}$ c) $\frac{12}{16}$
4 A $\frac{3}{7}$ and C $\frac{15}{35}$
B $\frac{2}{5}$ and F $\frac{6}{15}$
D $\frac{15}{24}$ and E $\frac{5}{8}$

25 Ordering fractions

1 a) $\frac{1}{3}, \frac{1}{2}, \frac{5}{6}$
b) $\frac{3}{5}, \frac{2}{3}, \frac{11}{15}$
c) $\frac{5}{24}, \frac{1}{4}, \frac{2}{6}, \frac{3}{8}$
d) $\frac{1}{4}, \frac{2}{5}, \frac{13}{20}, \frac{7}{10}$
e) $\frac{2}{5}, \frac{1}{2}, \frac{7}{10}$
f) $\frac{3}{4}, \frac{7}{9}, \frac{5}{6}$
2 a) $\frac{1}{3}$
b) $\frac{5}{6}$
c) $\frac{7}{10}$
d) $\frac{3}{5} = \frac{18}{30}$ and $\frac{9}{15} = \frac{18}{30}$
Yes, Jeannie is right.

26 Adding and subtracting fractions

1 a) $\frac{5}{11}$ b) $\frac{5}{10} = \frac{1}{2}$ c) $\frac{13}{15}$ d) $\frac{13}{24}$
e) $\frac{2}{9}$ f) $\frac{14}{15}$

2 $1 - \frac{5}{8} = \frac{8}{8} - \frac{5}{8} = \frac{3}{8}$

3 $\frac{1}{2} + \frac{1}{5} = \frac{7}{10}$, orange juice = $1 - \frac{7}{10}$
$= \frac{10}{10} - \frac{7}{10} = \frac{3}{10}$

27 Mixed numbers, improper fractions and reciprocals

1 a) $\frac{19}{5}$ b) $\frac{19}{2}$ c) $\frac{23}{3}$ d) $\frac{83}{3}$

2 a) $2\frac{4}{5}$ b) $3\frac{2}{3}$ c) $3\frac{5}{9}$ d) $6\frac{3}{4}$

3 a) $13\frac{4}{5}$ b) $5\frac{4}{11}$ c) $4\frac{4}{7}$ d) $1\frac{1}{6}$
e) $5\frac{7}{10}$ f) $20\frac{7}{12}$

4 a) $\frac{11}{7}$ b) $\frac{34}{2}$ c) $\frac{4}{3}$ d) $\frac{8}{5}$

28 Multiplying and dividing fractions

1 a) $\frac{3}{20}$
b) $\frac{14}{81}$
c) $\frac{4}{21}$
d) $\frac{21}{40}$
e) $\frac{8}{18} = \frac{4}{9}$
f) $\frac{20}{45} = \frac{4}{9}$

2 a) $\frac{13}{33}$
b) $\frac{9}{40}$
c) $\frac{11}{12}$

3 a) 1 $a\frac{b}{c}$ 3 ÷ 2 $a\frac{b}{c}$ 5 =
or 1 $a\frac{b}{c}$ 2 ÷ 3 $a\frac{b}{c}$ 5 =
b) 2 $a\frac{b}{c}$ 5 ÷ 1 $a\frac{b}{c}$ 3 =
or 3 $a\frac{b}{c}$ 5 ÷ 1 $a\frac{b}{c}$ 2 =
c) 5 $a\frac{b}{c}$ 3 ÷ 1 $a\frac{b}{c}$ 2 =
or 2 $a\frac{b}{c}$ 3 ÷ 1 $a\frac{b}{c}$ 5 =
d) 3 $a\frac{b}{c}$ 2 ÷ 1 $a\frac{b}{c}$ 5 =
or 5 $a\frac{b}{c}$ 2 ÷ 1 $a\frac{b}{c}$ 3 =

29 Calculating fractions of whole numbers

1 a) 9 litres b) 12 grams c) £32
d) 20 hours e) £1.35 f) £15

2 a) 20 3-bedroom houses
b) 12 4-bedroom houses

30 What is a percentage?

1 a) $\frac{1}{10} = 0.1$
b) $\frac{1}{4} = 0.25$
c) $\frac{3}{4} = 0.75$
d) $\frac{3}{10} = 0.3$
e) $\frac{1}{20} = 0.05$
f) $\frac{7}{10} = 0.7$
g) $\frac{2}{25} = 0.08$
h) $\frac{3}{20} = 0.15$

2 Pairs: A and D, B and G, C and H, E and F

31 Calculating percentages

1 a) 6 hours b) 40 cm c) 9 kg
d) $38 e) £13.50 f) 24 minutes

2 a) £4.56 b) 11.25 km
c) 22.1 grams d) £415.80

3 a) 8 students b) 6 students

32 Expressing a number as a percentage of another number

1 % reptiles, Osney Zoo:
$\frac{56}{400} \times 100 = 14\%$
% reptiles, Norham Zoo:
$\frac{45}{250} \times 100 = 18\%$
Norham Zoo has the bigger proportion of reptiles.

2 % boys, Mrs Alter's class:
$\frac{14}{32} \times 100 = 43.75\%$
% boys, Mrs Scott's class:
$\frac{12}{30} \times 100 = 40\%$
Mrs Alter's class has the bigger proportion of boys.

3 % dog walkers, Bridge Park:
$\frac{28}{80} \times 100 = 35\%$
% dog walkers, Rock Park:
$\frac{55}{125} \times 100 = 44\%$

% dog walkers, East Park:
$\frac{36}{96} \times 100 = 37.5\%$
a) Rock Park had the biggest proportion of dog walkers.
b) Bridge Park had the smallest proportion of dog walkers.

33 Converting between fractions, decimals and percentages

1 a) $0.21 = \frac{21}{100} = 21\%$
b) $0.53 = \frac{53}{100} = 53\%$
c) $0.79 = \frac{79}{100} = 79\%$
d) $0.06 = \frac{6}{100} = \frac{3}{50} = 6\%$
2 a) $\frac{11}{50} = 0.22 = 22\%$
b) $\frac{7}{10} = 0.70 = 70\%$
c) $\frac{23}{25} = 0.92 = 92\%$
d) $\frac{57}{75} = 0.76 = 76\%$
3 a) $2\% = \frac{2}{100} = \frac{1}{50} = 0.02$
b) $32\% = \frac{32}{100} = \frac{8}{25} = 0.32$
c) $72\% = \frac{72}{100} = \frac{18}{25} = 0.72$
d) $55\% = \frac{55}{100} = \frac{11}{20} = 0.55$
4 Pairs: A and F, B and H, C and G, D and E

34 Rounding to the nearest whole number, 10 or 100

1 a) 57 b) 2 c) 13 d) 108
2 a) 30 b) 70 c) 380 d) 40
3 £56.20, £63.12 or £55
4 a) 800 b) 300 c) 3800 d) 100

35 Approximating answers to calculations

1 a) $30 \div 6 = 5$
b) $2 \times 200 = 400$
c) $800 \div 4 = 200$
d) $9 \times 40 = 360$
e) $(2 - 1) \times 50 = 1 \times 50 = 50$
f) $(10 + 10) \div 5 = 20 \div 5 = 4$
g) $(60 + 40) \div 20 = 100 \div 20 = 5$
h) $(100 - 50) \times 3 = 50 \times 3 = 150$
2 $30 \div 6 = 5$ CDs
3 $5 \div 1 = 5$
$5 \times 3 = 15$ chocolate bars

36 Understanding unitary method

1 a) 9 cm b) 10×9 cm = 90 cm
2 a) $100 \div 5 = 20$ packets
b) $20 \times 40 = 800$ packets
3 £7.70

37 What is a ratio?

1 a) 8 : 6
b) 6 : 15
c) 35 : 5
d) 32 : 36
e) 12 : 18
f) 30 : 48
2 2 : 1 = 6 : 3, so 3 lemons
3 For every 1 litre blue, 4 litres yellow, 5 litres in total:
a) 4 litres blue
b) 16 litres yellow, 20 litres in total
c) 8 litres blue, 32 litres yellow, 40 litres in total

38 Algebraic expressions

1 a) $3s$ b) $q - t$ c) $7y + z$
2 a) $2n$ b) $n + 1$ c) $n - 2$

39 Simplifying expressions

1 a) $7j$ b) $5k - 4i$ c) $13e$
d) $17a - 3 + 2b$ e) $5x + 5y$
f) $10c + 20$
2 $x + 4x + 3x + \frac{1}{2}x = 8\frac{1}{2}x$

40 What is a formula?

1 16
2 4
3 $z - 4$
4 a
5 $\times 6$
6 22
7 2
8 $\frac{b}{3} + 4$
9 $\div 6$
10 $\times 5$

41 Substitution

1 a) £55 b) £75 c) £50
2 a) 37 b) 52
3 a) 10 b) 1
4 a) 28 b) 36
5 a) 33 b) 18

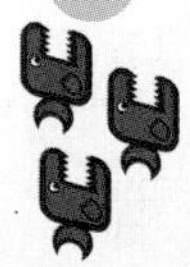

42 Solving equations

1 a) –4
b) × 11
c) ÷ 5
d) ÷ 6 + 1
e) + 9 × 3
f) × 4 – 6

2 a) $r = 5$
b) $m = 5$
c) $p = 20$
d) $d = 9$
e) $c = 2$
f) $a = 6$
g) $z = 7$
h) $b = 5$
i) $n = 6$

43 More equations

1 $p + 8 = 12, p = 4$
2 $10t - 9 = 31, t = 4$
3 $10q - 6 = 14, q = 2$
4 $8s + 20 = 100, s = 10$
5 $12 + 6x = 60, x = 8$
6 $10 + 7y = 52, y = 6$
7 $5n - 22 = 13, n = 7$
8 $6f + 18 = 30, f = 2$
9 $-1 + 11j = 21, j = 2$
10 $4 + 5r = 19, r = 3$

44 Using equations to solve word problems

1 a) $z + 2z = 27$,
$3z = 27, z = 9$
2 $4n + 3 = 35, n = 8$
3 $2p - 3 = 57, p = 30$

45 What is an inequality?

1 a) $a \geq 6$
b) $b < 9$
c) $c \leq 10$
d) $5 > d$

2 a) 2, 3, 4, 5
b) 1, 2
c) 4, 5, 6
d) –1, 0, 1, 2
e) –1, 0, 1, 2, 3
f) –3, –2, –1, 0

3 a) $r \leq 4$
b) $c > 8$
c) $j \leq 20$

46 Understanding number patterns

1 a) rule: + 3, next number: 17
b) rule: × 2, next number: 80
c) rule: ÷ 2, next number: 2
d) rule: + 5, next number: 29
e) rule: ÷ 5, next number: 1
f) rule: – 4, next number: 6

2 a) 2 b) 4 c) 16 d) 8

47 Finding the nth term

1 a) $6n$ b) $9n$ c) $7n$ d) $2n + 1$
e) $4n - 3$ f) $6n - 2$ g) $3n - 1$
h) $7n + 2$

2 a) 5th term = 30, 10th term = 60
b) 5th term = 45, 10th term = 90
c) 5th term = 35, 10th term = 70
d) 5th term = 11, 10th term = 21
e) 5th term = 17, 10th term = 37
f) 5th term = 28, 10th term = 58
g) 5th term = 14, 10th term = 29
h) 5th term = 37, 10th term = 72

48 Reading and plotting coordinates

1 A (2, 3)
B (–2, 1)
C (1, –2)

49 Mappings

1

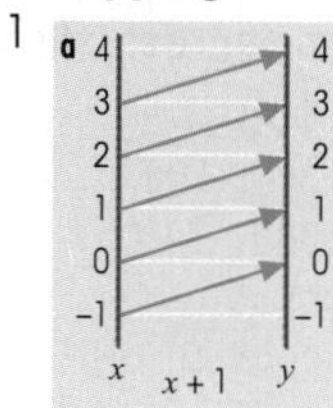

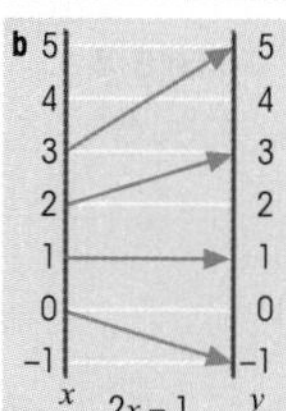

2 You might have 3 pairs from:
a) (–1, 0) (0, 1) (1, 2) (2, 3) (3, 4)
b) (–1, –3) (0, –2) (1, –1) (2, 0) (3, 1)

50 Drawing straight-line graphs by finding points

1 a) $y = x - 2$

x	0	2	4
y	–2	0	2

b) $y = x + 2$

x	–1	0	2
y	1	2	4

c) $y = \frac{1}{2}x - 1$

x	–2	0	2
y	–2	–1	0

2 a

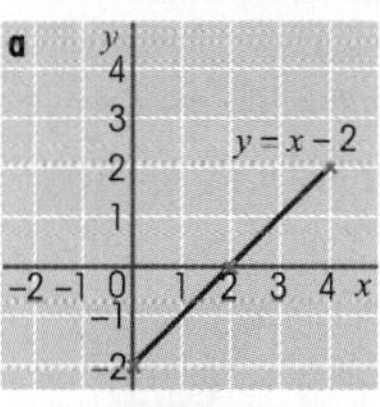

b

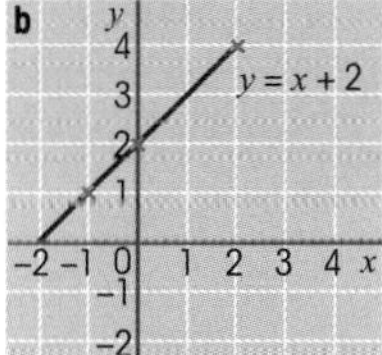

c

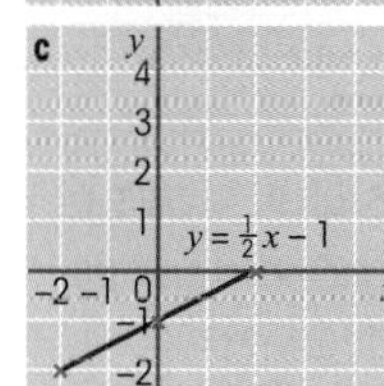

3 a

$y = x - 1$

b

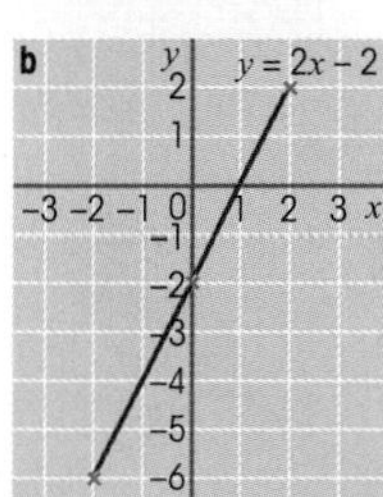

51 Gradient

1 a) 1 b) $-\frac{2}{3}$ c) $\frac{3}{2}$

2 a) $\frac{25}{100} = \frac{1}{4}$

b) $\frac{5}{100} = \frac{1}{20}$

c) $\frac{20}{100} = \frac{1}{5}$

52 Drawing straight-line graphs by finding gradient and intercept

1 a) gradient = 4, intercept = 1

b) gradient = 2, intercept = –3

c) gradient = 3, intercept = 2

d) gradient = 1–2, intercept = –2

e) gradient = –1, intercept = 4

f) gradient = –3, intercept = 2

2

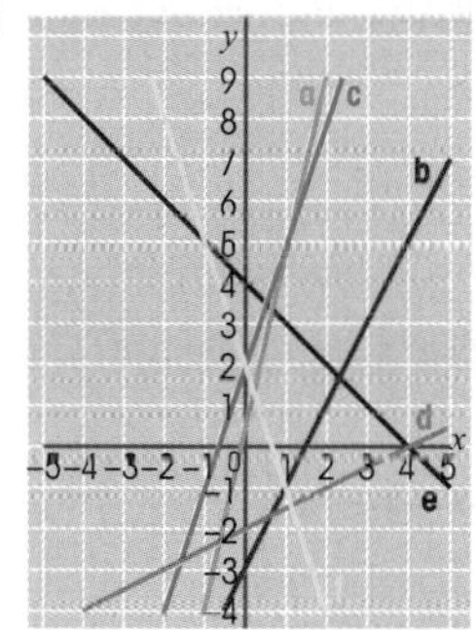

53 Finding the equation of a straight-line graph

1 a) gradient = 2, intercept = –2

b) gradient = 1, intercept = 0

c) gradient = $\frac{-1}{2}$, intercept =1

d) gradient = –2, intercept = 4

e) gradient = – 3 –2 intercept = –3

2 a) $y = 2x - 2$

b) $y = x$

c) $y = \frac{-1}{2}x + 1$

d) $y = -2x + 4$

e) $y = \frac{-3}{2}x - 3$

54 Parallel straight-line graphs

1 a) C b) D c) A d) B

2

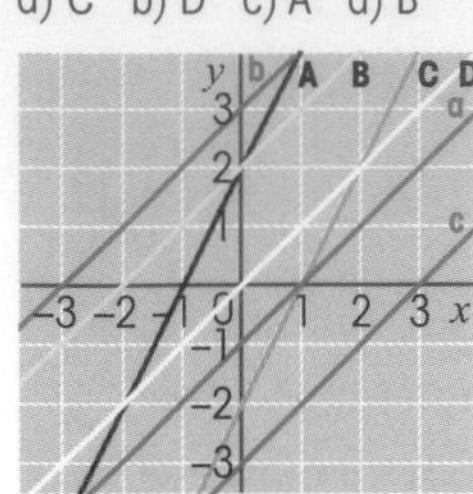

55 What is an angle?

1 a) acute b) reflex c) obtuse
d) reflex e) acute f) reflex

2 a) 112° b) 206°
c) 325° d) 80°

56 Measuring angles accurately

1 145°
2 18°
3 149°
4 331°

57 Drawing angles accurately

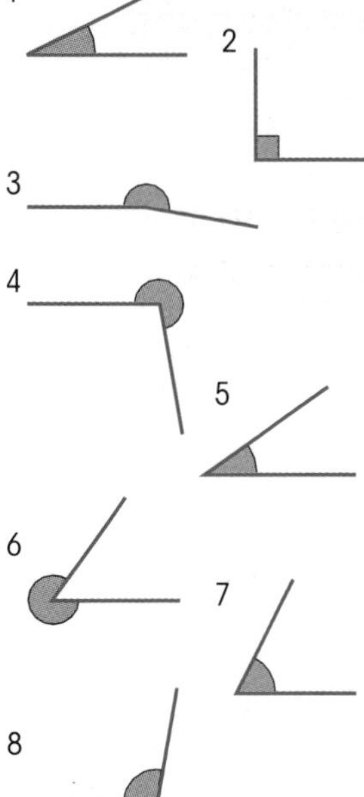

58 Angles on a straight line and angles around a point

1 a) 70° b) 90° c) 46° d) 64°

2 $x + x + 40 + 2x = 360$
$4x + 40 = 360$
$x \rightarrow \times 4 + 40 \rightarrow 360$
$360 \rightarrow - 40 \div 4 \rightarrow x$
$x = 80°$

59 Angles made by intersecting straight lines

1 75° (alternate angles)
2 39° (opposite angles)
3 108° (alternate angles)
4 62° (corresponding angles)

60 Two-dimensional shapes and three-dimensional solids

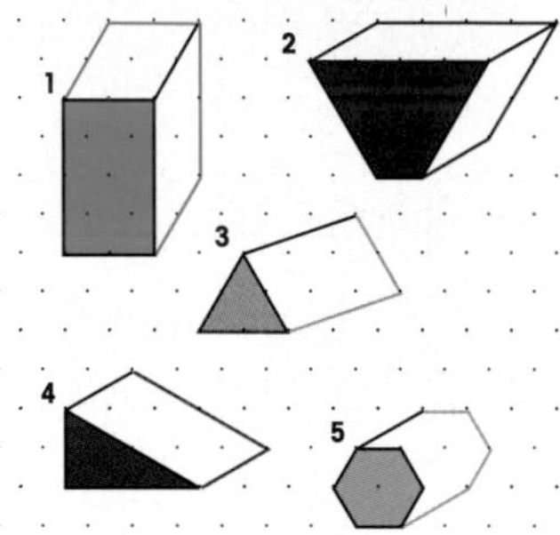

61 Two-dimensional views of three-dimensional solids

1 a) top (ii) front (iii) side (ii)
b) top (iii) front (i) side (i)
c) top (i) front (ii) side (iii)

2 You might have drawn:

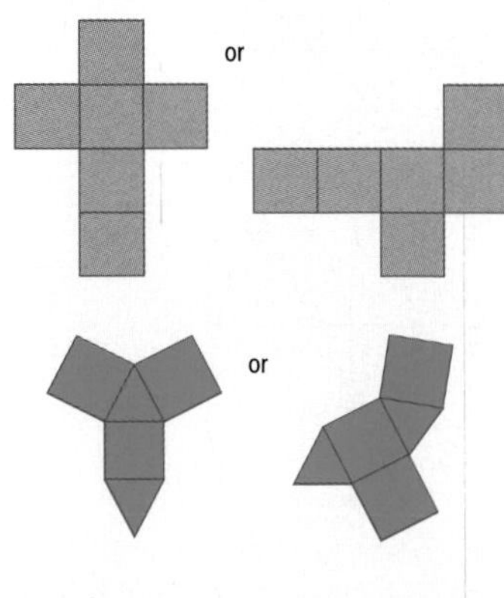

62 What is a polygon?

1 not a polygon
2 irregular polygon
3 regular polygon
4 irregular polygon
5 quadrilateral and irregular polygon
6 irregular polygon
7 not a polygon
8 regular polygon
9 regular polygon
10 irregular polygon
11 irregular polygon
12 quadrilateral

63 Quadrilateral properties

1 a) true b) true c) false d) true
e) false f) false

64 Interior angles of polygons

1

shape	no. of sides	interior angle
square	4	90°
rectangle	4	90°
equilateral triangle	3	60°
regular octagon	8	135°

65 Exterior angles of polygons

1

shape	interior angle	exterior angle
regular hexagon	120°	60°
regular octagon	135°	45°
regular nonagon	140°	40°
regular decagon	144°	36°

66 Circles

1 a) arc
b) diameter
c) sector
d) radius
e) circumference
2 a) 6 cm b) 12 mm c) 2.4 cm
3 a) 2 cm b) 5 cm c) 3.5 mm

67 Reflective symmetry

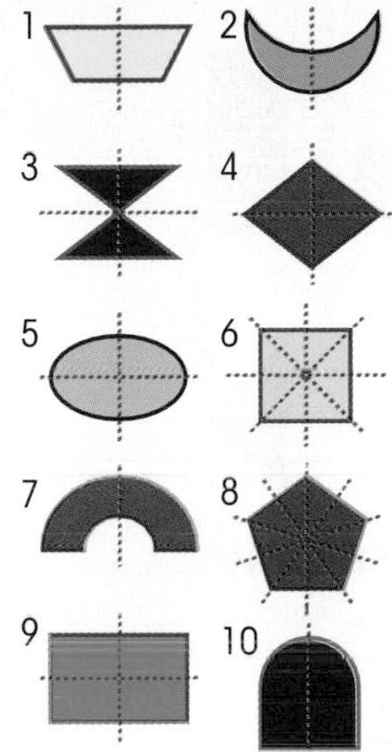

68 Rotational symmetry

1 a) 3 b) 4 c) 4 d) 8 e) 1
2 a) 2 b) 2 c) 4 d) 1 e) 2 f) 2
g) 2 h) 2

69 Congruent shapes

1 (a) and (f), (c) and (e), (b) and (i),
(d) and (j), (g) and (h)

70 Translation

1 a) shape T and shape W
b) shape Q
c) shape V
2 a) 6
b) Q
c) 4
d) 2 down, 2 right
e) 3 right, 2 up

71 Enlargement and similar shapes

1 a) M
b) 2
c) 2
d) 3
2 R and T, U and X

72 Drawing enlargements of shapes

1

A

2

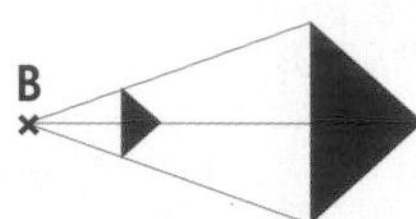

73 Units of measure

1 a) 4.1 °C
  b) 5 km
  c) 3 lb and 7 oz
  d) 6 pints
  e) 0 °F
  f) 1 ml
2 a) A and G
  b) B and D
  c) F and H
  d) C and E
  e) A, B, C and F

74 Converting units of measure

1 $96 \div 16 = 6$ lb
2 $1550 \div 10 = 155$ cm
3 $70 \div 14 = 5$ stones
4 $415 \div 100 = 4.15$ m
5 $25 \times 1000 = 25\,000$g
6 $36 \div 12 = 3$ feet
7 $10 \times 14 = 140$ lb
8 $1.8 \times 100 = 180$cm

75 Reading scales accurately

1 a) 5 g b) 2.5 mm c) 100 ml
  d) 1 °C e) 22 °C f) 30 g
  g) 100 ml h) 30 cm

76 Approximate metric and imperial equivalents

1 10 miles = $10 \times 1.6 = 16$ km
2 90 cm = $90 \div 30 = 3$ feet
3 4 litres = $4 \div 0.5 = 8$ pints
4 13 kg = $13 \div 6.5 = 2$ stones

77 Conversion graphs

1 a) 3 litres b) 4.5 litres c) 8 pints
  d) 5 pints
2 a) 16 km b) 5 miles c) 24 km

78 What is perimeter?

1 13 cm
2 12 cm
3 5.5 cm
4 5.8 cm
5 5.1 cm
6 18 cm
7 8.2 cm
8 19.3 cm
9 9 cm
10 8.6 cm

79 Finding the circumference of a circle

1 21.98 cm
2 25.12 cm
3 18.526 cm
4 19.468 cm
5 19.468 cm
6 29.83 mm

80 What is area?

1 10 units squared
2 11 units squared
3 13 units squared
4 7 units squared
5 $9\frac{1}{2}$ units squared
6 11 units squared

81 Using formulae to find area

1 $7 \times 2 = 14$ cm^2
2 $\frac{1}{2} \times 5 \times 3 = 7.5$ cm^2
3 $\frac{1}{2} \times 6 \times 4 = 12$ cm^2
4 $\frac{1}{2}(9 + 3) \times 5 = 30$cm^2
5 $6 \times 6 = 36$ cm^2
6 $7 \times 9 = 63$ cm^2
7 $7 \times 6 = 42$ cm^2
8 $\frac{1}{2}(0.6 + 3.4) \times 1.5 = 3$ cm^2

82 Finding the area of a circle

1 a) $3.14 \times 3 \times 3 = 28.26$ cm^2
  b) $3.14 \times 2 \times 2 = 12.56$ cm^2
  c) $3.14 \times 3.5 \times 3.5 = 38.465$ cm^2
2 a) circumference = 3.14×14
  = 43.96 cm
  area = $3.14 \times 7 \times 7 = 153.86$ cm^2
  b) circumference = 3.14×17
  = 53.38 cm
  area = $3.14 \times 8.5 \times 8.5$
  = 226.865 cm^2

c) circumference = 3.14 × 11
= 34.54 cm
area = 3.14 × 5.5 × 5.5
= 94.985 cm^2

83 What is volume?

1 20 units cubed
2 8 units cubed
3 9 units cubed
4 9 units cubed

84 Using formulae to find volume

1 $4 \times 4 \times 2 = 32$ cm^3
2 $1.5 \times 6 \times 8 = 72$ cm^3
3 $5 \times 20 \times 10 = 1000$ mm^3
4 $3.5 \times 3.5 \times 8 = 98$ cm^3

85 Finding loci

1 1 cm represents 1 m

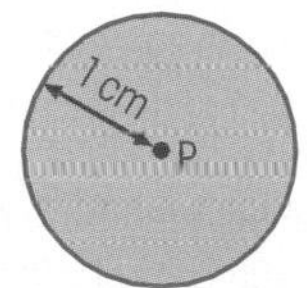

2 a)

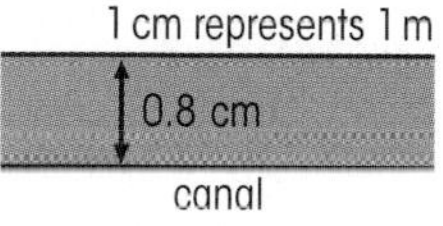

b)

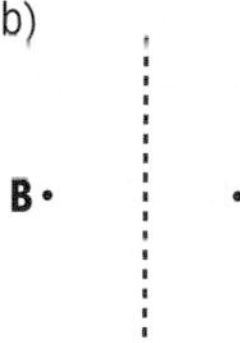

86 Tallies and frequency tables

1 a) The kind of books people like

type of books	tally	frequency
fiction	~~////~~ ~~////~~ /	11
biography	//	**2**
cookery	~~////~~ /	**6**
gardening	~~////~~ ///	8
arts	///	3

b) The days people like to visit the library

days	tally	frequency
Mon	//	2
Tue	~~////~~ //	7
Wed		0
Thu	~~////~~	**5**
Fri	////	**4**
Sat	~~////~~ ~~////~~ //	12

2 The number of books people tend to borrow

number of books	tally	frequency
0	/	1
1	~~////~~	5
2	~~////~~ ~~////~~ //	12
3	////	4
4	~~////~~	5
5	///	3

87 Grouped data

1 number of books

number of books	tally	frequency
1–5	~~////~~ ////	9
6–10	~~////~~ //	7
11–15	///	3
16–20	/	1
21–25	/	1

88 Bar charts

1 a) gym
b) 8
c) 7 + 10 + 5 + 8 + 6 = 36

2 Survey of time spent at Cornhead Fitness Centre

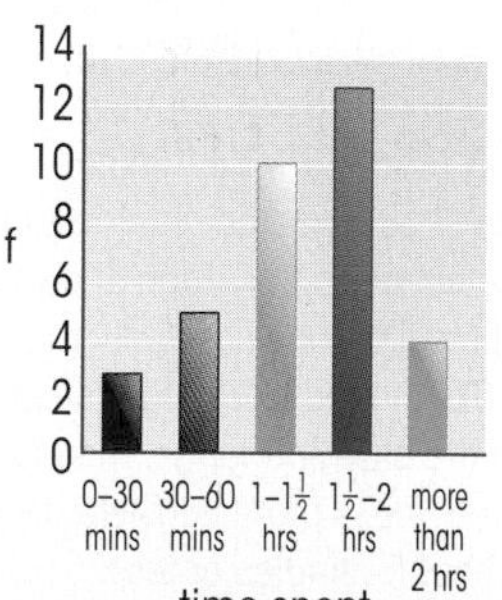

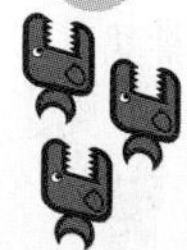

89 Drawing and interpreting line graphs

1 Rick
2 Rob fell over or stopped to tie his shoe lace.
3 5 minutes
4

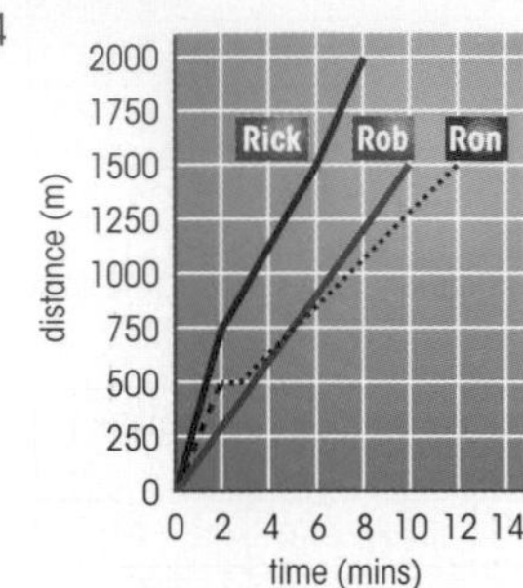

90 Interpreting pie charts

1 a) 216 ÷ 6 = 36
b) 216 ÷ 12 = 18
c) $\frac{1}{4}$
d) 216 ÷ 4 = 54
e) $\frac{1}{2}$
f) 216 ÷ 2 = 108

91 Mode

1 a) 23 b) 12 c) 6
2 a) 4 b) 5

92 Median

1 a) 17 b) 9 c) 22
2 a) 14 b) 9 c) 11.5

93 Mean and range

1 Red-line mean = 4.6 minutes
Blue-line mean = 4 minutes
Green-line mean = 10 minutes
Brown-line mean = 5.6 minutes
2 Red = 6 – 2 = 4 minutes
Blue = 9 – 0 = 9 minutes
Green = 12 – 8 = 4 minutes
Brown = 16 – 0 = 16 minutes
3 Freda should get the red-line tube, since although the mean shows that the blue-line tube is slightly more reliable, the red-line range is smaller than the blue-line range. Therefore, the red line is more consistently late by about 5 minutes or less.

94 Interpreting scatter diagrams

1 a) increases b) decreases
or a) decreases b) increases
c) negative
2 a) no
3 a) increases b) increases
or a) decreases b) decreases
c) positive

95 Drawing a line of best fit

1

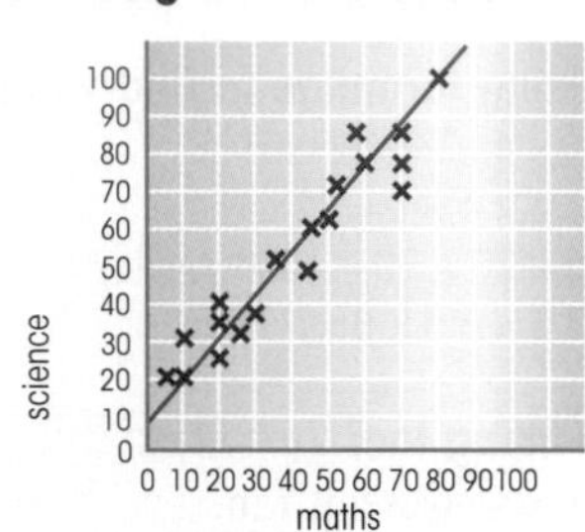

2 a) any percentage between 60% and 65% (it must be read correctly from your line of best fit)
b) any percentage between 58% and 62% (it must be read correctly from your line of best fit)

96 What is probability?

1

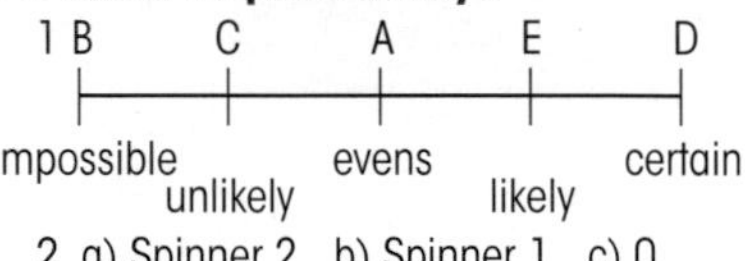

2 a) Spinner 2 b) Spinner 1 c) 0

97 Calculating probability

1 a) $\frac{1}{12}$
b) $\frac{1}{11}$
c) $\frac{2}{31}$
2 a) $\frac{1}{4}$
b) $\frac{3}{4}$
c) $\frac{2}{4} = \frac{1}{2}$
d) $\frac{2}{3}$

98 Mental methods

1 a) 370.4 nautical meters
b) 648.2 nautical meters
2 £104.66

99 Preparing for a mental maths test: tier 3–5

1 4 metres
2 7
3 14
4 45°
5 37 minutes
6 32 cm
7 86 %
8 $2y + y + 3y = 6y$
9 5 001 642
10 630
11 $7p - q = 27$
12 4 pints
13 40 girls
14 1 p
15 $\frac{2}{4}$ or $\frac{1}{2}$

100 Preparing for a mental maths test: tier 4–6

1 6
2 340
3 1400 cm
4 $\frac{4}{5}$
5 30
6 108°
7 $3x - 1 = 23$
8 557
9 $\frac{4}{7}$
10 $5x - 3$
11 0.027
12 5 g 7 g 11 g 6 g 5 g
13 440 yen
14 60 cm^3
15 30 cm